# Quick & Easy
# WordStar 2000
## Janet Crider

**HPBooks®**
**Publisher:** Rick Bailey
**Editorial Director:** Theodore DiSante
**Technical Consultant:** Roylan Mosley
**Art Director:** Don Burton
**Book Design and Assembly:** Leslie Sinclair
**Typography:** Cindy Coatsworth, Michelle Carter
**Director of Manufacturing:** Anthony B. Narducci

D1528906

**Published by HPBooks, Inc.**
P.O. Box 5367, Tucson, AZ 85703  602/888-2150
ISBN: 0-89586-408-8  Library of Congress Catalog No. 85-80116
©1985 HPBooks, Inc.  Printed in U.S.A.

# Part I
# Introduction

This book teaches you about word processing with WordStar 2000. By working through examples of typical word-processing tasks, you will learn about the basic and advanced features of this powerful program. If this is your first exposure to word processing, read this introductory section carefully. If you are already familiar with the original WordStar program or another word-processing program, scan this introductory section as a review.

**HOW TO USE THIS BOOK**

This book supplements the manuals and disk tutorials provided by MicroPro in your WordStar 2000 package. Here's how this book is organized:

Part I of this book introduces you to the *commands,* the keystrokes you type from the keyboard to make WordStar 2000 do what you want.

Part II provides the examples you use to learn about the power of WordStar 2000. To explore all of the features of WordStar 2000, I recommend that you work through all of the examples. They are arranged in an order of increasing complexity, building on things already discussed up to that point.

Part III introduces you to the advanced features of WordStar 2000 Plus. These include TelMerge telecommunications, MailList, and StarIndex.

# Introducing 1
# WordStar 2000

WordStar 2000 is a *word processor*—a computer program that allows you to type, store and print text of all kinds. This includes letters, memos, reports, contracts, book manuscripts, and research papers at home, in school, or in an office. The *documents* may be short or long, printed once or used repeatedly.

The ability to quickly and easily *edit*—add to, delete or revise what you have typed—is one of the outstanding advantages of using a word processor rather than a typewriter or pen and paper. You can change some portions of the document while keeping acceptable portions unchanged. You can change the document as much as you wish. In addition, you can *format* the document, specifying the design of the printed page. Format characteristics include items like top, bottom and side margins, tabs, line spacing, and typeface choices.

## WHAT YOU NEED WITH WORDSTAR 2000

To use WordStar 2000 you need an IBM PC—or compatible—computer with at least 256K RAM. This means that the computer can hold about 256,000 characters in its memory. Some of the memory is consumed by the WordStar 2000 program, and some is used by document text. As necessary to clear space in memory, WordStar 2000 refers to the disk to load more into its memory or to write information to the disk.

WordStar 2000 also requires two double-sided floppy disk drives or one double-sided drive and a *hard,* or *fixed disk.* A hard disk holds many times more information than a single floppy disk.

A hard disk will hold all of the WordStar 2000 programs, eliminating the need to remove and replace the program floppy disks to perform certain functions. The hard disk is also recommended because it allows the computer to locate information more quickly. Because of the size of the WordStar 2000 program, you may experience some delays as the computer locates another part of the WordStar 2000 program. Even so, a hard disk is not essential to using the many features of WordStar 2000.

## CAPABILITIES OF WORDSTAR 2000

WordStar 2000 possesses the powerful features required in today's state-of-the-art word processor. Commands are letter-coded to be *mnemonic*—meaning the letter codes will make it easy to remember the word they represent. For example, to edit a document you will press the E key when the Opening Menu is on the screen. To have WordStar 2000 print you press the P key. In each case, the letter code is the first letter of the command you want to execute. **Commands**—If you need to have some commands explained along the way, WordStar 2000 will do so when you press the *Help* key, Function key F1. The mnemonic equivalent of this is depressing the Control key then pressing the G key. The G stands for Get help. This and other WordStar 2000 commands can be given two different ways—with two or three keystrokes using the regular typing keys, or with a Function key.

The Control key, abbreviated as *Ctrl* on your keyboard, is used for many WordStar 2000 commands. Alone it does nothing, but when coupled with one or two other keys, such as G, you can give a command. From here on out, I'll use a *caret* (^) to represent the Ctrl key because that's what WordStar 2000 does. So when you see something like ^G, for example, hold down the Ctrl key and then depress the G key. As described earlier, this command tells WordStar 2000 to get help.

**Menus**—WordStar 2000 also uses *menus,* lists of choices, displayed in the upper portion of the screen. As a menu in a restaurant lists your culinary choices, a menu in WordStar 2000 lists your command choices. You communicate most of your command choices to WordStar 2000 by selecting an item from a menu. In some cases you will simply type one letter, the mnemonic representation of the command you want to give. At other times you will type a letter while depressing Ctrl, shown on the menu with a caret (^) preceding the letter. The menu will tell you exactly what you need to type.

Sometimes, after selecting an item from the menu, you'll see the screen change to display a *submenu,* another list of choices. As you learn WordStar 2000 commands by using this book, you'll become familiar with all of the menus. **Editing Features**—As you type, the *wordwrap* feature automatically begins a new line of text when the current line is filled. This eliminates the need to press the Return key—it's the key with the engraved down-and-left arrow that acts like the carriage return on a typewriter. You press Return—also sometimes called *Execute* or *Enter*—only when a *new* line must begin, for example, after each line of the inside address on a letter or at the end of a paragraph.

You will appreciate the *Undo* command. It restores the most recently deleted text. For example, if you inadvertently delete something from your document, WordStar 2000 is ready to cooperate when you change your mind. Letting the word processor retype the deleted text saves you a lot of typing time and reduces frustration.

As you add and delete text, WordStar 2000 automatically rearranges, or *reforms,* the lines to fit the formatted margins.

WordStar 2000 can also do five arithmetic functions while you're typing—addition, subtraction, multiplication, division and exponentiation. This is like having a calculator within the word processor.

If you have ever wished you could see another part of the document you're editing, or even refer to a different document, WordStar 2000's *windows* let the wish come true. You can display up to three different portions of text on the screen simultaneously, each in its own window. You can move from window to window, and copy or move *blocks*—marked sections of text—from one window to another.

So-called *key glossaries* store and recall frequently used words or phrases, eliminating repetitive typing. For example, if you type the word *condominium* frequently, you could use the letter c in the key glossary to represent the whole word. Then instead of typing *condominium,* you use the short-hand keystroke c and press Esc. Then you sit back and watch as WordStar 2000 immediately writes *condominium.* You can use this amazing feature for many different tasks—such as giving your company or department name in documents or to type the closing for business correspondence.

**Formatting Features**—WordStar 2000 lets you create and store page formats that define page layout for printing. Several standard formats are provided with the program. You can also quickly prepare additional formats, store them on a disk, and use them repeatedly with different documents.

What you see on the screen shows many of the formatting features in place. WordStar 2000 displays indented text, hyphenated words, line breaks, and page breaks so you won't get any surprises when the document prints. Text can be formatted *justified* so the text aligns on the right margin as well as on the left. Or, it can be *unjustified* so the right margin is ragged like a typewriter produces it.

You can also set the top, bottom and side margins, and tabs. *Headers* and *footers*—one or more lines of text automatically printing at the top and bottom of pages respectively—are easy to add. You can use them to print page numbers or repeating text.

**Printing Features**—You will also see some of the special print features on the screen as they will print. Boldfaced text appears brighter than normal text. Text to be printed underlined looks that way on the screen. Some computers may show boldface and underline in *reverse video*—in which the colors of the text and the background switch—depending on the configuration of your particular computer. Regardless of how your computer makes the distinction, you will see that section of text marked for special treatment.

To underline or print text in boldface, you simply insert a command at the point the special feature begins and ends. WordStar 2000 will also overprint characters, a feature you use to add accent-type marks into text.

To add a professional touch to a document, you can print it in several columns on the page like a newspaper or magazine format.

You may continue working with WordStar 2000 while a document prints, saving you valuable time. You can interrupt the printer, then resume or cancel the printing if you need to make additional editing changes.

WordStar 2000 lets you print using the different typestyles—sometimes called *fonts*—available on your printer. You can also specify the *pitch*—the number of characters printed per inch.

Your document can be printed *proportionally spaced*—allocating more space to an m or w than to an i or l, just as in this sentence. Generally *letter-quality printers,* those with removable print wheels or thimbles, can print text proportionally. Many *draft-quality* or *dot-matrix* printers, which create characters by printing small dots, are not capable of proportional spacing.

If you need to quickly address a single envelope, prepare a mailing label, or complete a form, you will appreciate WordStar 2000's *typewriter mode.* Text typed at the keyboard is sent directly to the printer without saving it on disk.

Another powerful feature of WordStar 2000 is MailMerge, also called the *merge printer.* It is commonly used to combine, or *merge,* a name-and-address list with a standard letter to produce personalized documents. You can use the same name-and-address list to print labels or envelopes to accompany the letters.

## OTHER FEATURES

WordStar 2000 can sort lists in a document alphabetically or numerically, in ascending order—A to Z or 1 to 100, respectively—or descending order—Z to A or 100 to 1. This provides a quick way to put an office phone directory in alphabetical order or a page of addresses in zip-code order.

If spelling isn't one of your strengths, let CorrectStar check your document with nearly *75,000 words* built into its list. You can check a single word or paragraph as you type, or check the entire document when it is finished. CorrectStar makes suggestions for correct spelling based on phonetic rules. So even if you typed the first letter of a word wrong but it "sounds" right, CorrectStar can figure it out. For example, you could spell *pneumonia* as *newmonya.* Because your spelling sounds like the word you want, CorrectStar will recognize and recommend the intended word!

WordStar 2000 will also keep track of footnotes for you, renumbering them as necessary while you edit. Then it will print them in order at the end of the document.

# *Getting Started* 2
# *With WordStar 2000*

Now let's get started with learning how to really use WordStar 2000, a truly amazing word processor. Part I of this book introduces you to using WordStar 2000 basics. You will learn about the most common commands and procedures. Part II builds on these basics by providing useful examples you will create with WordStar 2000.

## THE KEYBOARD

An important part of feeling comfortable with the WordStar 2000 commands is familiarity with the arrangement of keys on the keyboard. The accompanying illustration shows the IBM PC keyboard. If you are using a comparable computer or an IBM PC AT, the keys may be arranged and labeled differently.

Function keys F1 through F10 are used alone and with the Shift key to give commands to WordStar 2000. The commands executed by these 20 combinations can be changed during the installation procedure if you desire—as discussed in the next section. The number keys on the top row of the keyboard become command keys when the *Alt* key is depressed.

The third group of keys used to give commands are on the numeric keypad. It's at the right side of the keyboard. You use the Arrow keys—the 4, 8, 6 and 2 keys—to move the *cursor,* the small, blinking line that travels around the screen. The cursor marks the place where the text you type will appear, or where the command you give will take effect. Some of these Arrow keys can be used with the Ctrl key to make bigger cursor movements. These are discussed later, when you need them.

The *Esc* key lets you leave or "escape from" a menu on the screen. This way, it becomes a way of cancelling a command before it is executed.

You press the *Return* key to let WordStar 2000 know that you are done typing some information requested as part of giving a command. When you are typing a document, pressing the Return key tells WordStar 2000 to begin a new line.

The *Tab* key is marked with left- and right-pointing arrows and is just above the Ctrl key. Use the former to move the cursor from one tab setting to the next, performing like a tab key on a typewriter. The Spacebar acts as it does on a typewriter, inserting blank spaces between words or sentences.

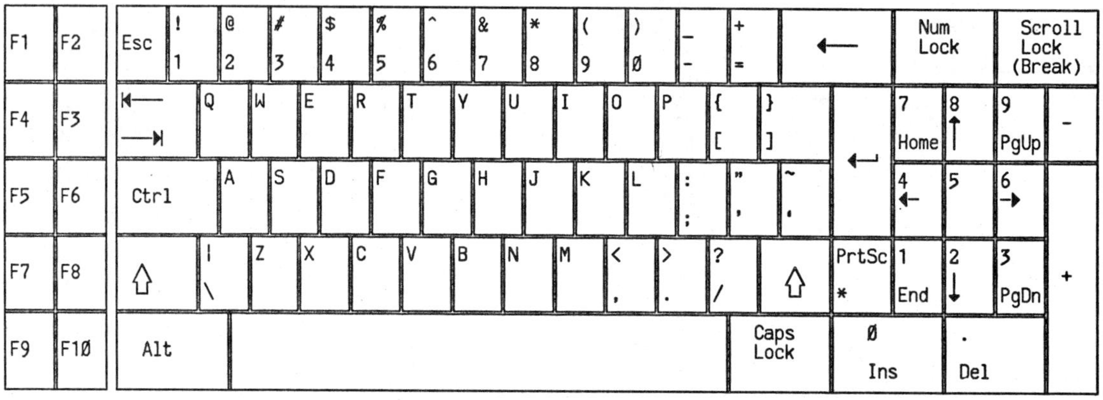

Fig. 2-1/The keyboard of an IBM PC looks like this.

## INSTALLING WORDSTAR 2000

Your new copy of WordStar 2000 must be *installed,* or set up, for your computer. This is essential—the program will not run without it. If you will be using WordStar 2000 on a computer with two disk drives, several disks must be *formatted.* This prepares them for storing information and programs.

During the first part of the installation procedure, the WordStar 2000 programs are copied onto the formatted floppy disks or onto the hard disk. Refer to the *Installation Guide* booklet that comes with WordStar 2000 for details on installing the program.

The second part of the installation guides you through a set of questions that sets up the program for your computer and printer. At this time you can specify *default* settings, the set of commands that will automatically be in effect when you use WordStar 2000. The *Installation Guide* refers to these as "Advanced Modifications."

For example, you can redefine the commands that are executed by the Function keys and set the colors that identify various print characteristics, such as boldface and underline, if you have a color monitor.

## LOADING THE WORDSTAR 2000 PROGRAM

Two sets of instructions are given here for loading—called *booting*—WordStar 2000. Use the first set if you have two floppy disk drives and the second if you are using a hard disk.

**If You Have Two Floppy Disk Drives**—To begin working on your first document, you need three disks:

1) Your DOS disk, version 2.0, 2.1 or 3.0. This can also be called the *start-up* disk. (*DOS* stands for Disk Operating System. DOS rhymes with *boss.)*

2) The *installed working copy* of program disk 2. Do *not* use the original copy of the disk that came with WordStar 2000! When the installation is complete, it should be put away in a safe place in case you need to make a new working copy.

3) A *formatted disk* that will be used to store the documents you type with WordStar 2000. This could be called the *data disk.*

Insert the DOS disk in Drive A, the left or upper drive, and turn on the computer. Type the current date if you are prompted to do so, then press Return. Next, type the time in military fashion and press Return. To bypass either or both questions, press Return rather than typing anything. When the prompt A> appears on the screen, remove the DOS disk and insert the copy of program disk 2 into Drive A. Insert the data disk into Drive B.

When you see the prompt, type

WS2

in either uppercase or lowercase letters and press Return. The Opening Menu appears on the screen.

**If You Have a Hard Disk**—To load WordStar 2000 in a hard-disk computer, put the DOS disk in Drive A—the left or upper slot—when you turn on the computer. Type the current date and time as in the sample format if you are prompted to do so. Press return after typing. To bypass either or both questions, press Return rather than typing anything. When the hard-disk prompt C> appears, type

WS2

using either uppercase or lowercase letters and press Return. The Opening Menu will be displayed on the screen.

A hard disk also offers another option for loading the WordStar 2000 program. The computer will boot from the hard disk, seeking for the necessary DOS programs put there when the hard disk was set up for use, if you leave the door on Drive A open when you turn on the computer. This forces the computer to go to Drive C for its information. When the hard-disk prompt appears on the screen, type

WS2

and press Return.

# 3 Creating Documents & Stored Formats

This chapter covers two important aspects of working with WordStar 2000—beginning work on a document and designing, assigning and changing stored formats. It might seem that you should create a document before formatting it. However, because of the way WordStar 2000 creates formats and stores them in format files, it is best—though not essential—to create the format before beginning work on the document. So, first we will create a format, then create a document.

## THE OPENING MENU

The Opening Menu is shown in Figure 3-1. This appears on the screen when the computer has loaded the WordStar 2000 program. You will come back to this menu frequently for changing tasks.

This menu offers choices like E for Edit/create, P for Print, G for Get help, and Q for Quit. To select any of the tasks, you simply press the bold letter that begins the desired option.

**Changing Default Drive**—If you are using a computer with two disk drives, you need to tell WordStar 2000 where you want to store the format files and documents you create. To do this you must change the *default drive* to specify the *storage drive.* Until you make a change, Drive A is the default drive if you are using a computer without a hard disk. However, because the disk in Drive A already holds all of the WordStar 2000 programs, practically no space remains for storing additional documents. If you are using a computer with a hard disk, Drive C is the default drive.

OPENING MENU - 1 of 2

| | | |
|---|---|---|
| Edit / create | Print | Get help |
| Remove | Copy | Quit |
| Directory / drive | Key glossary | |
| Move / rename | Typewriter mode | |
| Spelling correction | Format design | |

Fig. 3-1/WordStar
2000 Opening Menu.

Press a highlighted letter or Spacebar for more choices.

To change the default drive type

D

on the Opening Menu to select the Directory/drive option. WordStar 2000 then asks

Change directory or disk drive to?

If you are using a computer with two floppy disk drives, change the default drive by typing

B:

and pressing Return. The Opening Menu then reappears on the screen.

If you are using a hard disk and you want to set the default to a drive other than Drive C, type

D

on the Opening Menu. Then type

D:

or another letter that coincides with the setup of the hard disk and press Return.

You can specify the default drive by typing the letter of the desired drive before the filename when naming the document or format. I'll show this a bit later.

## WORKING WITH STORED FORMATS

In the next section of this chapter, you will learn to create a new document and name it. When you have done this, WordStar 2000 asks

Name of Format to Use?

You must give the name of a format to begin work on a document. The *format* is a file stored on the disk that prescribes how the pages of the document will appear when printed. Because you are asked to provide the name of a format file, it is most convenient if the format is created before you begin work on a document. That's why I'm discussing formats first.

When you edit an existing document, WordStar 2000 doesn't prompt for the name of the format. Rather, the format most recently assigned to it is automatically used.

**Creating a Format**—Creating a format requires some advance planning. You need to have some idea of how the printed document should fit onto the page so that you can respond to the questions posed by WordStar 2000 when setting up the format file. Creating the format before giving the Edit/create command on the Opening Menu makes it possible to select the desired stored format from the list when WordStar 2000 prompts for it.

To create a format file, you must be at the Opening Menu. (If you have already selected one of the commands from the Opening Menu and now want to cancel the command to return to the Opening Menu, press Esc to make the Opening Menu reappear.) To design a format, type

`F`

to select the Format design option.

WordStar 2000 then displays the Choose a Name Screen and asks

`Format or formatted document name?`

Like a document, the format file must have a name. The name can be up to eight characters long and can be any combination of letters and numbers. The name cannot have spaces. For example, WORKTEXT is a valid format name, but WORK TEXT isn't. After typing the valid format filename, type the characters

`.FRM`

so you would see

`WORKTEXT.FRM`

and press Return. WordStar 2000 now recognizes that a file named WORKTEXT with the *extension* .FRM contains format instructions. If a file by this name doesn't already exist, WordStar 2000 assumes you are creating a new format. If you give the name of an existing format, you can change its contents. Later, you will create and name a document WORKTEXT and use this format file to format the text.

After naming the format, you respond to a series of questions to create the format. WordStar 2000 supplies an answer to each question. Press Return to keep this default answer, as shown on the screen. You will then see the next question.

Following are the questions WordStar 2000 asks, followed by a brief explanation about the responses you can give. To create the WORKTEXT.FRM file, press Return to accept the default on each question:

**Font to use?**—As mentioned earlier, *Font* refers to typestyle and *pitch,* or size, of the characters. The default and possible choices for your printer are shown on the screen. Make the selection by typing the number or highlighting your choice and pressing Return. Move the highlight bar with the Arrow keys in the numeric keypad.

**Line height (spacing)?**—Line height or line spacing sets the number of lines that will print per vertical inch of the page. The default is 6.00—six lines per inch—or single spacing. Other choices include 8.00 (tighter text with eight lines per inch), 4.00 (one-and-one-half spacing), 3.00 (double spacing), and 2.00 (triple spacing).

**How many lines in the top margin?** — Default is 6, which provides a one-inch top margin if text is single-spaced. If you change line height to double spacing and want a one-inch top margin, change the setting to 3.

**How many lines in the bottom margin?** — The top-margin defaults and guidelines apply.

**Right margin in what column?** — Default is 65, meaning that text will be formatted with a 65-character line, assuming a pitch of 10 characters per inch. In other words, the printed text line will be 6-1/2 inches long.

If pitch changes, the line of text will still be 6-1/2 inches if the right margin remains at 65. WordStar 2000 calculates the number of characters that will fit into the lines using the selected pitch. Unlike some word processors, you don't need to reset the right margin when character size changes.

**Set a tab stop at every n columns — enter a number for n** — Default is 5, meaning that tabs are automatically set every 5 spaces between the set margins. Use this command to set tabs at evenly spaced intervals. Other tabs can be set when you are working on a document. If you want no tabs set, type

Ø

**Number of lines per page?** — Default is 66, which assumes the default single line spacing. If the line spacing option is changed, the number of lines per page must also be changed. Note that this number specifies the number of lines of *text* on a page, not the total number of lines available on the page. For example, if line spacing is 3.00 (double spacing), you must change the number of lines per page to 33.

**Even page offset in columns?** — Page offset determines the number of blank spaces between the left edge of the paper and the first printed character when the left margin is set at 1. Default is 10 spaces. For example, if the page offset remains at 10 and you change the left margin to 5, the first character of a line will print in the 16th space from the left edge of the paper. This question lets you set the page offset for even-numbered pages.

**Odd page offset in columns?** — This question sets the page offset for odd-numbered pages. The discussion for even-page offset applies. The two are controlled separately to permit two-sided copying and binding.

**Text Justified or Ragged-right? (J/R)** — Default is J for Justified, aligning text at the right margin as well as the left, as in a newspaper. Typing R for Ragged-right results in the right edges of the lines being uneven, like the pages of this book.

**Automatic hyphenation on? (Y/N)** — Default is Y, which allows WordStar 2000 to automatically hyphenate words. The hyphens inserted are *conditional,* or *soft,* hyphens. They are used and printed only on the condition that they fall at the end of the line and are used to divide the syllables of a word.

**Use form feeds when printing? (Y/N)** — Default is Y, which lets WordStar 2000 give the printer an "advance-to-top-of-next-page" signal. Some printers require the N response to print page breaks correctly or to prevent blank pages between printed pages. If you don't know which choice your printer requires, accept the default. Later, if documents print incorrectly, change this setting.

**Underline between underlined words? (Y/N)** — Default is Y, which underlines characters and spaces between underlined characters. Change the setting to N to underline only words but not the spaces between words, producing a broken underline.

**Display page breaks? (Y/N)** — Default is Y, which shows the page breaks on the screen. You will find the default the most convenient setting.

**Page numbers: Centered, Left, Right, Alternating, or None? (C/L/R/A/N)** — Default is N, for None.

**Final Direction** — When you have gone through the list of questions, you must tell WordStar 2000 what to do with the format changes you have typed. Three choices are shown at the top of the screen. You type S to Save the choices, E to Edit the list again to make more changes, or A to Abandon the format.

In this case, type

S

to save the changes. The Opening Menu reappears.

Now that you have designed format, you are ready to create a document. Actually typing and using the text will begin in the next chapter.

## CREATING AND USING A DOCUMENT

You begin work on a document from the Opening Menu. Type

E

the highlighted letter of the Edit/create option. The Opening Menu disappears and WordStar 2000 displays the Choose a Name Screen. WordStar 2000 asks

Document to edit or create?

Like designing a format file, before you can start work on a new document, you must give it a name. Type

WORKTEXT

Then press Return.

Another way to begin work on a document is to type the document name when you load the WordStar 2000 program. When the prompt A> appears on the screen, type

WS2 B:ELEMENTS

to begin work on a document named *ELEMENTS* that will be stored on the disk in Drive B. Remember that you can type the filename in either uppercase or lowercase letters. WordStar 2000 converts the name to all caps when it is displayed in the *directory,* a list of all the files on a disk.

You can also use this method on a hard disk. When the C> prompt appears, type

`WS2 ELEMENTS`

to create the document and store it on the C drive of the hard disk.

Typing the filename when you load the WordStar 2000 program lets you bypass the Opening Menu. If the document named ELEMENTS already exists on the specified drive, it will appear on your screen.

Read through the following paragraphs to learn about the alternatives available to you when naming a document. You will use the WORKTEXT document in this chapter and the next.

**Naming a New Document**—Like a format filename, the name of a document can be up to eight characters long, comprised of any combination of letters and numbers. It can include a limited number of punctuation characters such as the hyphen but cannot include spaces. The period is reserved for separating the filename from the *extension,* an optional group of up to three characters that follow the filename. Remember that you used the extension .FRM earlier to identify a format file.

Examples of valid filenames include LETTER, MEMO1, JOHNSON.LTR, 12-3-85.RPT, B, and B.DOC. The filename can be typed in uppercase or lowercase letters, but WordStar 2000 converts them to all uppercase letters.

You cannot use the extension .BAK. WordStar 2000 reserves this extension to identify a backup file, which stores the previous version of a document on a disk. More on this later when saving typed documents is discussed.

An alternative to changing the default drive mentioned earlier in this chapter is to include the storage drive when naming the document. You can specify where the document will be stored by typing the drive letter followed immediately by a colon and the filename. For example, typing

`B:WORKTEXT`

will store the document named WORKTEXT on the disk in Drive B. The document C:WORKTEXT will be stored on Drive C on your hard disk. If you did not change the default drive at the beginning of this chapter, delete what you have typed using the Backspace key and type

`B:WORKTEXT`

or

`C:WORKTEXT`

When the document name appears as you want it, press Return.

**Using Directories**—If you are using a hard disk, you can give some further instructions when WordStar 2000 asks `Document to edit or create?` You can set up *directories* to organize and group the documents you create. When you name the document, you can specify the directory as well as name a document.

Think of the document as a file folder inside a file drawer, the directory. Related documents are stored in the same directory—the same file drawer—but each is in its own folder or document file.

For example, you may have a directory named *CONTRACTS* for storing all documents relating to contracts. To begin work on a document named *ALLIANCE.BID* that is to be stored in the CONTRACTS directory, type

```
CONTRACTS\ALLIANCE.BID
```

Refer to the DOS manual for further information about setting up and using directories on your hard disk.

**Selecting a Stored Format**—After you name the document and press Return, WordStar 2000 asks

```
Format to use?
```

All of the files with the FRM extension stored on the active disk drive—the default drive or the changed default drive—are shown on the screen. The WordStar 2000 program disk includes five commonly used formats. You will see these names on the screen if they are stored on the active drive. Use the Arrow keys on the numeric keypad to move the highlight to the WORKTEXT.FRM format. Then press Return. This format file will be used to determine how the WORKTEXT document will be printed.

Keep in mind that the selected format will "remain" with the document. It is not necessary for you to remember the name of the assigned format, nor will you go through the format design each time you want to work on the WORKTEXT document.

However, it is possible to change the format assigned to a document after it has been stored on the disk. There's more on this in the next chapter, after you type and save the WORKTEXT document.

## SAVING A DOCUMENT

As you type, the text exists only in the memory of the computer. If you turned your computer off, or if the electricity flow to your computer failed, everything you had typed would be lost. Before this shocking discovery throws you into a panic, let's look at how you can tell WordStar 2000 to save what you have typed on the disk.

The following four choices are shown on the screen after you type ^Q.

```
Save changes            Abandon changes
Continue after saving   Print after saving
```

Three commands tell WordStar 2000 to store the document, and one says "forget about it."

**Quit and Continue**—After you type ^Q and the choices appear on the screen, press C to save the document and continue working on it. Another way to give this ^QC command is to press Alt-3.

Doing this commands WordStar 2000 to save the document and then let you continue working on it. The cursor stays in position on the screen so you can resume editing at the same spot when the document is stored. You might think of this as an update command, updating the copy of the document on the disk with the most recent changes.

I can't overemphasize that you should get into the habit of saving a document regularly. A power failure lasting a fraction of a second can clear everything in your computer's memory, including all of the changes you have made in your document since the last Save command. The document as it was last saved, however, generally remains intact on the disk during a power failure.

It is not unreasonable to give the Quit and Continue command every 10 to 20 minutes. This seems to be very often—and it is. But you may find that you have breaks in your work at frequent intervals. Before you get up to get a cup of coffee, type the Quit and Continue command. When a phone call interrupts your work, type the command.

As your document gets longer, the save takes more time. However, the few additional seconds hardly compare with the time you would spend retyping and re-editing the lost document.

**Quit and Save**—You type

`^QS`

or Alt-1 to Quit and Save the document. This means that you are done working on the document during this session. You would type this command before going to lunch, at the end of the day, or when you want to create or edit another document. After executing the command, WordStar 2000 puts the Opening Menu back on the screen.

**Quit and Print**—If you have completed the document and are now ready to print it, type

`^QP`

or Alt-4 to Quit and Print. When the document is saved, you see the *Print Decisions Screen.* There's more on this in a later chapter.

**Quit and Abandon**—This command allows you to leave a document without saving the most recent editing changes. You type

`^QA`

or Alt-2. If you have made any changes in the document, WordStar 2000 displays

`This document has been changed. Abandon anyway? (Y/N) N`

If you type Y, WordStar 2000 abandons the document without storing the most recent revisions on the disk. To change your mind about abandoning the document, press Return to accept the default No answer.

You might use this command following a demonstration of WordStar 2000's features to some friends which resulted in changes to your document that you don't want to keep. Give the Quit and Abandon command and the document will be preserved as it was previously stored on the disk. If you created a new document for this demonstration, WordStar 2000 "forgets" that the document was ever created and you won't see it listed on the directory of files.

## CHANGING THE FORMAT OF AN EXISTING DOCUMENT

Once a format is assigned to a document, you can easily change it. With the Opening Menu on the screen, type

F

to select the Format item just like you did to create a format. WordStar 2000 asks

Format or formatted document name?

Type the name of the document whose format is to be changed. You are again given the opportunity to respond to the series of format questions used when creating a format file. This time, the format you create does not affect any of the stored format files. Only the format of the named document is changed.

## EDITING AN EXISTING DOCUMENT

When you have created and stored several documents on this disk or directory, you will see a list of the names after typing E from the Opening Menu. All of the documents are listed on the lower part of the Choose a Name Screen. The first one in alphabetical order or the one last edited during this session is highlighted. To edit the highlighted document, simply press Return.

If you want to edit one of the other documents listed, use the Arrow keys on the numeric keypad to move the highlight to the desired document. Then press Return. The next thing you see is the beginning of the requested document.

# *Basics Of Editing* 4

In this chapter you will learn about some of the most common editing tasks and their commands—typing, inserting and deleting text, and moving the cursor. Although the discussion here doesn't explain *all* of the editing commands available in WordStar 2000, these are the ones you will use most when working on documents. You'll practice these more when you apply them to working examples in Part II of this book.

You remember from an earlier chapter that you type E from the Opening Menu to edit or create a document. The document you named was WORKTEXT, using the stored format named WORKTEXT.FRM. You are now ready to begin typing a document.

## THE EDITING MENU

The Editing Menu shown in Figure 4-1 is displayed at the top of the screen while you edit. Notice that the highlighted letters on the Editing Menu are preceded by a caret, ^. WordStar 2000 uses the caret to represent the Ctrl key on your keyboard. When the caret precedes a character—^C, for example—you know to depress the Ctrl key while you type the letter C. You can type the C either uppercase or lowercase.

Many of the commands you select from the Editing Menu will display another menu, called a *submenu.* The Editing Menu serves as a guide to most of the menus and commands that can be given to WordStar 2000.

**Setting the Menu Display**—Once you are familiar with the WordStar 2000 commands (it may happen before you finish this book!), you may not need the

*E*diting Menu on the screen while you type. You may prefer to use the entire screen for text. You can do this by changing the *help level* to bypass some or all of the menus. To do this, type

^ GG

or press F1 twice. Then press the highlighted letter of your choice on the screen: A so All menus are displayed, S so only Submenus are displayed, or N so No menus are displayed. You will always see the Opening Menu, regardless of the help level you select.

The Status and Ruler Lines, two lines at the top of the screen, provide important information about the cursor position, the tabs and the margins set for the document. These lines remain on the screen even when the Editing Menu is removed.

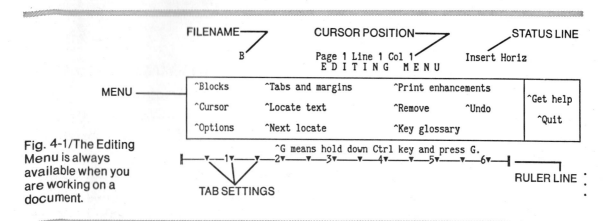

Fig. 4-1/The Editing Menu is always available when you are working on a document.

**Getting Help**—WordStar 2000 has built-in help menus that explain how to use commands. For example, type

^G

or press F1 when the Editing Menu is on the screen to see WordStar 2000 display the first of five *help screens.* These explain what you see on the editing screen, what each of the options on the Editing Menu let you do, how to move the cursor through the document, and which commands the function keys perform.

Help menus are always available even if you set the help level to suppress some or all of the other menus. Type the "get help" command and "page through" the help screens by pressing the Spacebar. When you're finished, press the Esc key to return to your document. The help screens provide different information if you request help when another of the menus is on the screen.

## TYPING AND INSERTING TEXT

You can now type text and give commands that affect the text. The cursor identifies where the next character you type will be placed. Most WordStar 2000 commands also take effect at the cursor.

You'll see that typing with WordStar 2000 is very much like typing on a typewriter. Type the following line, pressing the Spacebar to create the space between words:

`George Washington lived at Mount Vernon.`

You can easily erase a mistake and type it again. To delete a typing error just to the left of the cursor, press the Backspace, the key with the left-pointing arrow on the top row of the keyboard. To remove a character at the cursor, press the Delete key, which may be named *Del* on your keyboard and shares space with the decimal point on the numeric keypad.

Further, you can insert words between text that you already typed. Press the Left-Arrow key in the keypad until the cursor is on the *W* of *Washington.* (If pressing the key prints 4s rather than moving the cursor, press the Num Lock key once. This key switches the use of the keypad between typing numbers and using the Arrow keys.) Now type

`and Martha`

inserting the words between *George* and *Washington.* The sentence now reads

`George and Martha Washington lived at Mount Vernon.`

**Wordwrap**—As more words are added to the sentence, the line extends past the right margin setting. When this happens, WordStar 2000 automatically begins a new line. This feature is called *wordwrap.*

The only time you will press Return is when you require a new line to begin. For example, when typing several sentences in a paragraph, let WordStar 2000 wrap the lines for you, pressing Return only at the end of the paragraph so you can begin typing the next paragraph on the line below.

To add more words to the sentence and see wordwrap in action, press the Right-Arrow key until the cursor is resting on the period at the end of the sentence on the screen. Press the Spacebar once, then type

`overlooking the Potomac River in Maryland`

When the screen line fills, text automatically shifts—or wraps—to the next line. The period is pushed over as you type, putting it in place when the newly revised sentence is complete.

**Overtyping Text**—You now realize that Mount Vernon is in Virginia, not Maryland. One way of correcting this is to type over the incorrect word. Move the cursor to the *M* of *Maryland,* using the Arrow keys in the keypad.

Then press the Insert key once. It is marked *Ins* and shares the zero key of the keypad. The word *Insert* on the Status Line at the top of the screen changes to *Over.* When that word appears on the screen, anything you type will type over and replace any existing text. Now type

`Virginia`

Press the Insert key again to restore the insert condition. You have now made a correction in the sentence by typing over the incorrect word.

## MOVING THE CURSOR

You have already seen that moving the cursor is an important part of typing and editing text. You must be able to move the cursor to the place you want to type or remove text, moving it over text without erasing anything and without inserting undesired blank spaces between words.

**Arrow Keys**—Using the four Arrow keys on the keypad may be the easiest way—though not always the quickest way—to move the cursor through text. The Left-Arrow and Right-Arrow keys move the cursor a character to the left and right, respectively. The Up-Arrow and Down-Arrow keys move the cursor up and down a line, respectively.

The cursor's movement to the left and right is enlarged when you hold the Ctrl key down while you press the Left-Arrow or Right-Arrow keys. Typing Ctrl-Right Arrow moves the cursor to the first character of the next word. Typing Ctrl-Left Arrow moves the cursor to the beginning of the previous word, the word to the left.

**Cursor Menu**—Although at first glance you might think the foregoing commands give you enough options, WordStar 2000 offers an even larger array of choices for moving the cursor through a document. These are found on the Cursor Menu, which appears on the screen after you type ^C. (Remember, this means to hold the Ctrl key down while typing the letter C.)

There are actually two Cursor Menus. When the first one is displayed, press the Spacebar to see the second. Press the Spacebar again to return to the first one. To select one of the choices in the menu, simply press the highlighted letter. Notice that the caret does not precede the letter on the menu, so you can make a choice without pressing Control. Figure 4-2 shows the two Cursor Menus and Figure 4-3 summarizes all of the cursor-movement commands.

**Cursor-Movement Diamond**—WordStar 2000 users familiar with WordStar commands will feel at home with the cursor-movement diamond, *one of the few sets of commands common to both programs.* The cursor-movement diamond is a group of letter keys on the left end of the keyboard that move the cursor when you press Ctrl. It uses a few letter keys for commands, as summarized in Figure 4-4.

## DELETING TEXT

You have already learned about several ways to delete text. You can type over it or use the Backspace and Delete keys for removing characters one at a time. WordStar 2000 also offers commands for removing words, lines, paragraphs or larger marked sections.

The commands for deleting selected portions of text are found on the Remove Menu, displayed when you type ^R. Typical of WordStar 2000, the commands are mnemonic. For example, you type ^RW to Remove Word or ^RS to Remove Sentence. The Remove Menu is shown in Figure 4-5. The remove commands are summarized in Figure 4-6.

**Using Undo**—Inevitably, you will delete something from a document unintentionally. It may be something you have no way of replacing—such as

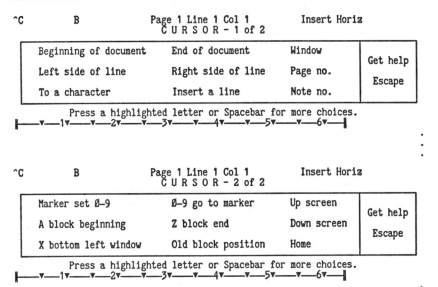

```
^C        B           Page 1 Line 1 Col 1        Insert Horiz
                        C U R S O R - 1 of 2

┌────────────────────────────────────────────────────┬──────────┐
│ Beginning of document   End of document      Window  │          │
│                                                      │ Get help │
│ Left side of line       Right side of line   Page no.│          │
│                                                      │ Escape   │
│ To a character          Insert a line        Note no.│          │
└────────────────────────────────────────────────────┴──────────┘
       Press a highlighted letter or Spacebar for more choices.
├──▼──1▼──── ▼──2▼──── ▼──3▼──── ▼──4▼──── ▼──5▼──── ▼──6▼──┤
```

```
^C        B           Page 1 Line 1 Col 1        Insert Horiz
                        C U R S O R - 2 of 2

┌────────────────────────────────────────────────────┬──────────┐
│ Marker set Ø-9          Ø-9 go to marker     Up screen│         │
│                                                      │ Get help │
│ A block beginning       Z block end        Down screen│         │
│                                                      │ Escape   │
│ X bottom left window    Old block position   Home    │          │
└────────────────────────────────────────────────────┴──────────┘
       Press a highlighted letter or Spacebar for more choices.
├──▼──1▼──── ▼──2▼──── ▼──3▼──── ▼──4▼──── ▼──5▼──── ▼──6▼──┤
```

Fig. 4-2/WordStar
2000 Cursor Menus.

# CURSOR-MOVEMENT COMMANDS

| Category | Command | Keystroke |
|---|---|---|
| Character Movement | Next character | Right Arrow or ^D |
| | Previous character | Left Arrow or ^S |
| | To a character | ^CT plus character |
| Word Movement | Next word | ^Right Arrow or ^F |
| | Previous word | ^Left Arrow or ^A |
| Line Movement | Previous line | Up Arrow or ^E |
| | Next line | Down Arrow or ^X |
| | Beginning of line | ^Home or ^CL |
| | End of line | ^End or ^CR |
| Screen Movement | Next screen | PgDn or ^CD |
| | Previous screen | PgUp or ^CU |
| | Top left of screen | Home or ^CH |
| | Bottom left of screen | End or ^CX |
| Block Movement | Beginning of block | ^CA |
| | End of block | ^CZ |
| Marker Movement | Set marker | ^CM and number |
| | Move to marker | ^C and number |
| Window Movement | Next window | ^CW or Shift-F3 |
| | Upper left of window | ^CH or Home |
| | Lower left of window | End or ^CX |
| File Movement | Beginning of file | ^CB or ^PgUp |
| | End of file | ^CE or ^PgDn |
| | Page of file | ^CP and number |
| | Footnote | ^CN and number |

Fig. 4-3

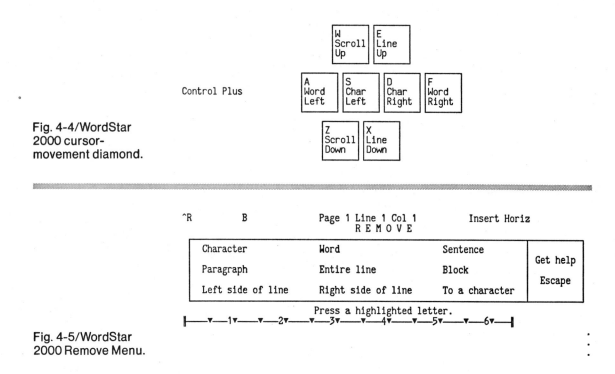

Fig. 4-4/WordStar
2000 cursor-
movement diamond.

Fig. 4-5/WordStar
2000 Remove Menu.

## REMOVE COMMANDS

| | | |
|---|---|---|
| Remove Character | Character left | Backspace Key |
| | At cursor | Delete Key or ^RC |
| Remove Word | Entire word | ^RW or F6 |
| Remove Line | Entire line | ^RE or Shift-F6 |
| | To left of cursor | ^RL |
| | To right of cursor | ^RR |
| Remove Sentence | Entire sentence | ^RS |
| Remove Paragraph | Entire paragraph | ^RP |
| Remove Marked Block | Entire block | ^RB or ^BR |
| Remove to Character | All between cursor and specific character | ^RT |

Fig. 4-6

one-of-a-kind information. Or it may be something less unique but still something you intended to leave in your document. This is one of the times the Undo command comes to your rescue. It "undoes" the most recent deletion command, retyping the text that was just removed.

To see how this works, position the cursor anywhere in the word *Potomac* in the sentence you typed earlier. Now type

^RW

or press F6 to Remove Word. The entire word disappears and the rest of the line moves to the left to close the gap. Notice that the entire word is deleted with this command, regardless of the cursor's position in the word.

Without moving the cursor, put *Potomac* back into the sentence by typing

^U

or by pressing F2 to Undo the deletion command. The sentence now reads just as it did before text was deleted:

```
George and Martha Washington lived at Mount Vernon overlooking
the Potomac River in Virginia.
```

You can also use Undo to move text to a different place in the document. For example, let's remove the words *in Virginia* and restore them after *lived* to make the sentence read

```
George and Martha Washington lived in Virginia at Mount Vernon
overlooking the Potomac River.
```

To do this, position the cursor on the *i* of *in* and type

^RR

to Remove Right side of the line. Now move the cursor to the *a* of *at* and give the Undo command by typing

^U

or pressing F2. Delete the period from the middle of the sentence—it was removed and restored with the commands you gave—and type one at the end of the sentence.

In this example, you delete all the text from the cursor to the end of the sentence. Another way to do this is by typing

^RT

to Remove To a character. WordStar 2000 prompts

```
Remove from cursor to what character?
```

Type a period to remove all text to the next period, which is the end of the sentence. The words can then be restored at a different place as with the other command. With the ^RT command, the period isn't removed. It stays in place, eliminating the need to delete the period from the middle of the sentence and add one to the end.

The Undo command restores text deleted with any of the commands on the Remove Menu except ^RC, Remove Character. Also, Undo does not restore text deleted with the Delete or Backspace Keys. Keep in mind that Undo restores only the most recently deleted text. If you want to use the command to move text—deleting it from one place and restoring it at another—press Undo before deleting any other text.

**If You Know WordStar**—If you are familiar with WordStar, you may find yourself automatically giving WordStar commands to delete text in WordStar 2000. Most of these commands evoke no response from WordStar 2000, or at least do nothing destructive.

For example, ^Y, the command used in WordStar to delete a line, is ignored by WordStar 2000. You will notice different functions performed by the Delete and Backspace keys. Figure 4-7 compares WordStar 2000 and the WordStar deletion commands.

## USING KEY GLOSSARIES

As described earlier, a *key glossary* provides a way of storing and recalling frequently used sections of text. You type the *key,* a shorthand version of the longer text, and let WordStar 2000 type the long form into the document. The keys and the longer text they represent are stored together in a *glossary,* named like other files and stored on the disk with the identifying filename extension KEY.

**Defining a Key Glossary**—Before you can use a glossary, you must define or create it. You can do this from the Opening Menu by typing *K,* or if in a document by typing ^K.

Let's say that you want to set up a glossary that types *George and Martha Washington* for you. Type

K

at the Opening Menu or

^K

in a document. A menu appears, with the following choices:

```
Define    Remove    Use another key file
```

Type

D

to Define a key that prompts WordStar 2000 to ask

```
Short form to define?
```

Now type the shorthand, or key, version of the glossary—the initials

```
GMW
```

## DELETION COMMANDS OF WORDSTAR & WORDSTAR 2000

| WordStar Command | WordStar 2000 Response | Comments |
|---|---|---|
| ^Y (delete line) | None | |
| ^T (delete word) | Displays Tab and Margin Menu | Press Esc to cancel command. |
| ^Q commands: | | |
| ^QY (delete to right side of line) | Displays Quit Menu | Press Esc to cancel command. |
| ^Q-Del (delete to left side of line) | Displays Quit Menu | Press Esc to cancel command. |
| ^G (delete cursor) | Displays Help Menu | Press Esc to cancel command. |
| Delete key | Deletes character at cursor | WordStar deletes character to left. |
| Backspace key | Deletes character left of cursor | WordStar moves cursor a character to left without deleting characters. |

Fig. 4-7

for example, and press Return.

The short form can be 1 to 15 characters long, a combination of letters and numbers. Although you can type the letters in uppercase or lowercase, WordStar 2000 will convert them all to uppercase for storing. You'll want to name the short form with as few characters as possible—it means less typing for you—yet with a name that will later be recognizable. In this case, you are using initials.

Next WordStar 2000 asks

`Long form?`

Type

`George and Martha Washington ^Q`

to enter and end the long form text. In this case, pressing Return doesn't end the entry as you might expect. Rather, the cursor would be moved to a new line so you could type more text.

The long form can hold up to 560 characters—seven lines of up to 80 characters each. It can include commands such as boldface or underline, discussed later. To type a command that uses the Ctrl key, type the caret literally with Shift-6 rather than pressing Ctrl. For example, the boldface command is usually typed ^PB or using F4. However, in the long form, you type Shift-^PB so you see

`^PB`

on the screen. Don't use Ctrl-PB or press F4 to include the boldface command in a long form.

WordStar 2000 will let you type other short forms now. When you are finished with all you want to create now, press Esc, which prompts WordStar 2000 to ask

`Should these changes be saved? (Y/N) N`

To save them type

`Y`

The key that you have defined must now be assigned to a glossary. WordStar 2000 asks

`Key file to use?`

Type

`GEORGE.KEY`

and press Return to complete the definition of the key glossary. Use the extension KEY so WordStar 2000 will recognize this as a key glossary file.

Later, while typing a document about George and Martha Washington, you might realize that you could use more keys to make your typing easier. You may want to add words and phrases like *Mount Vernon; Philadelphia, Pennsylvania; Alexandria, Virginia; Declaration of Independence;* and *the First Continental Congress* to the key glossary. Follow the steps above and give the name GEORGE.KEY as the key file to use for the long forms I just suggested.

One key glossary can store up to 20 different keys with their long forms up to a maximum of 2000 characters for the entire glossary. The key glossary is designed to store and recall relatively short sections of text. If you need to use longer portions of text, perhaps a page or several pages, use WordStar 2000's *block feature.* It is described in the next section.

**Listing Short Forms**—You can see a listing of all short forms stored in a glossary. To do this, type

`^KU`

Select the desired glossary from the directory shown on the screen by moving the highlight bar to it and pressing Return. Then type

`^KD`

This is the command to define another key. WordStar 2000 then displays all of the short forms already included in the current glossary.

**Separate Key Glossaries**—If you create several different kinds of documents, you may find it most convenient to define a separate key glossary file for each kind. For example, you will use the GEORGE.KEY file for the research you do relating to George Washington.

When writing a novel about Hawaii, you create NOVEL.KEY that stores the names of your characters, streets, buildings, cities and the like.

Finally, you can create CORRESP.KEY to store text used in correspondence, including a return address and the letter closing. Simply tell WordStar 2000 which KEY file you are using with the current document by typing ^KU, highlighting or typing the name and pressing Return.

You can set up many different key glossary files but you can access only one at a time. For example, while using GEORGE.KEY, WordStar 2000 will not recognize one of the short forms you stored in NOVEL.KEY. To use one of the NOVEL.KEY short forms, you would type ^KU and select NOVEL.KEY from the list of available key glossary files. Then to go back to using shortforms from the GEORGE.KEY glossary, you would type ^KU again and select GEORGE.KEY.

## WORKING WITH BLOCKS OF TEXT

Key glossaries allow you to store and recall relatively short sections of text. Use WordStar 2000's block feature to store and recall longer sections of text—several paragraphs, pages or multiple pages in length.

A *block* is a section of text marked for special treatment. Once marked, it can be moved to a new location in the same document; it can be copied to a new location in the same document or a new document; or it can be deleted. WordStar 2000 puts no limit on the size of a block—it can be one word, a sentence or paragraph, or 35 pages, for example.

Use the sentence about George and Martha to practice the block commands that follow. You will use the commands shown in the Block Menu of Figure 4-8.

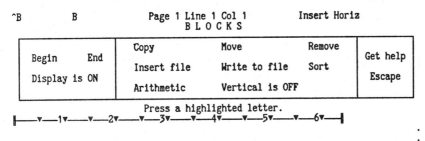

Fig. 4-8/WordStar 2000 Block Menu.

**Marking the Block**—To tell WordStar 2000 the block you wish to work with, you must mark it. First, position the cursor at the beginning of the section and type ^BB for Block Begin or press F9. You will see

`<B>`

on the screen. Then move the cursor to the end of the section and type ^BE for Block End or press Shift-F9. The entire marked section is highlighted on the screen. Only one section of text can be marked as a block at any given time.

**Moving the Block**—Once a block is marked it can be moved—taken from its original location and placed elsewhere in the document. To do this, position the cursor at the place the marked block is to go. Type ^BM for Block Move or press F10. The block remains marked after it is moved, so you could move it again by repositioning the cursor and repeating the block move command.

**Copying the Block**—A marked block can also be copied—left in its original location and duplicated in another place. The copied block will then appear twice in the document. After marking the block, position the cursor at the place in the document where the block is to be duplicated. Type ^BC for Block Copy or press Shift-F10. The newly copied block is still marked, making it possible to make another copy of the block by moving the cursor and repeating the command. You can copy and move blocks from one document to another by using windows, as described in the next section.

**Removing the Block**—A marked block can quickly be deleted with a single command. Type ^BR for Block Remove or ^RB for Remove Block. The text is taken out of the document and any text below it moves up to fill the gap. The marked text will be removed even if it is not visible on the screen.

Should you change your mind about the deletion, restore it with the Undo command—^U—or by pressing F2 before any other text is deleted. The text is reinstated at the cursor's position. Notice that this command can be used for moving text: mark the block, remove it, move the cursor, and give the Undo command. The block reappears at a new location.

**Writing the Block to a New File**—Once a block of text is marked, it can be stored in a new file. The block remains in the current document when it is copied into a new file. You could use this command to divide a long document into two files, or to save a frequently-used section of text that is too long to fit into a key glossary. These sections of text are often referred to as *boilerplate text.*

First, let's say that you are writing a novel and you typed the first two chapters in the same file. You now want to separate this document so chapter one is in one file and chapter two is in another. To create a new file and put chapter 2 in it, mark chapter 2 as a block. Then type

^BW

for Block Write. WordStar 2000 asks

File to write to?

You will type the name

CHAPTER2

for example, and press Return. You can write it to a different disk drive by preceding the filename with the intended drive:

B:CHAPTER2

or

C:CHAPTER2

Chapter 2 is still marked as a block so you can remove it from the current document by typing

^BR

or

`^RB`

leaving only the text of chapter 1.

As another example, let's assume that you have the responsibility for responding to travel and customer-service inquiries in a busy travel office. Before long, you notice that the letters are somewhat repetitious—you write the same paragraphs repeatedly. The ability to mix and match from a reservoir of paragraphs could meet most of your writing requirements. To do this, store each of the frequently used paragraphs as a separate document with the `^BW` command and recall them on demand.

**Recalling a Stored File**—To create a letter using stored paragraphs, position the cursor in the letter document where you want the paragraph to appear and type

`^BI`

for Block Insert. WordStar 2000 prompts

`Document to insert?`

Move the highlight bar to the name of the file or type the filename containing the first paragraph and press Return. The paragraph is inserted and immediately matches the format of the rest of the document. Once the paragraphs are inserted into the letter, they can be edited as necessary without affecting the stored paragraph.

The new files created with the `^BW` command are unformatted, meaning that the format assigned to the original document was not copied with it. However, commands such as boldface or underline stay with it when the block is written. You can edit the unformatted document, but it is inconvenient. No margins are in effect, so the lines extend far past the right edge of the screen.

You will also see some unusual characters in the text. One way to give CHAPTER2 a format is to create a new document, CHAP2 for example, select or design a format for it, and insert CHAPTER2 with `^BI`. When you recall a stored document, it assumes the format of the document into which it is inserted.

You will learn more about working with stored and repetitious text in a later chapter. You will also mark column or vertical blocks and use the sort and built-in mathematics capabilities of WordStar 2000 within marked blocks.

## USING WINDOWS

WordStar 2000 permits you to divide or split the screen into two or three *windows* on the screen so you can view parts of up to three different documents simultaneously. You can see up to two parts of the same document at the same time. You can move the cursor from one window to another, edit in each window, and move or copy marked text from one window to another.

You will find this feature helpful for several things. You can follow an outline in one window while you write the document in another window. Or you can refer to information from a second document while writing. The window command is found on the Options menu, shown in Figure 4-9.

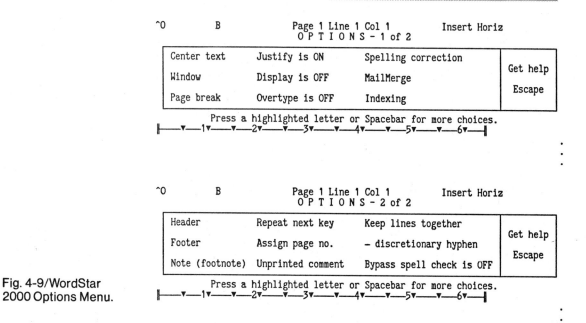

Fig. 4-9/WordStar
2000 Options Menu.

**Opening a Window**—To open a second window on the screen, type

^OW

for Option Window or simply press F3. WordStar 2000 asks you to specify which
document will be put in the new window:

Document to edit or create?

Type a new document name or select the document from the list shown on the
lower portion of the screen and press Return. The document you select can be the
same one you are currently editing, it can be an existing document stored on the
disk, or a new one. You will see the second window on the screen as shown in
Figure 4-10.

To open a third window, give the ^OW command again and select or type a
document name. Remember that you can have one document displayed in two
different windows but not in all three. The screen with three windows is shown in
Figure 4-11.

**Moving the Cursor Between Windows**—A bonus for using windows is the ability
to move the cursor from window to window—and even move text from one
window to another. To move the cursor to another window, type ^CW for Cursor
Window or press Shift-F3. The cursor moves from window to window in the order
they were created. For example, if the cursor is in the second of three
windows—the middle one on the screen—typing the ^CW command moves the
cursor to window three, the one lowest on the screen.

Give the command again to move the cursor to the first window, the original
document at the top of the screen. Typing ^CW again returns the cursor to the

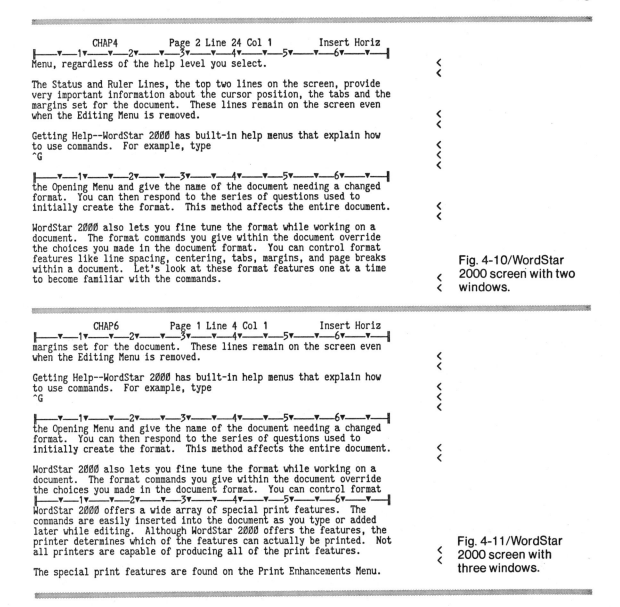

```
            CHAP4           Page 2 Line 24 Col 1          Insert Horiz
├────▼──1▼────▼───2▼────▼───3▼────▼───4▼────▼──5▼────▼───6▼────▼───┤
Menu, regardless of the help level you select.

The Status and Ruler Lines, the top two lines on the screen, provide
very important information about the cursor position, the tabs and the
margins set for the document.  These lines remain on the screen even
when the Editing Menu is removed.

Getting Help--WordStar 2000 has built-in help menus that explain how
to use commands.  For example, type
^G

├────▼──1▼────▼───2▼────▼───3▼────▼──4▼────▼───5▼────▼───6▼────▼───┤
the Opening Menu and give the name of the document needing a changed
format.  You can then respond to the series of questions used to
initially create the format.  This method affects the entire document.

WordStar 2000 also lets you fine tune the format while working on a
document.  The format commands you give within the document override
the choices you made in the document format.  You can control format
features like line spacing, centering, tabs, margins, and page breaks
within a document.  Let's look at these format features one at a time
to become familiar with the commands.
```

Fig. 4-10/WordStar 2000 screen with two windows.

```
            CHAP6           Page 1 Line 4 Col 1           Insert Horiz
├────▼──1▼────▼───2▼────▼───3▼────▼──4▼────▼───5▼────▼───6▼────▼───┤
margins set for the document.  These lines remain on the screen even
when the Editing Menu is removed.

Getting Help--WordStar 2000 has built-in help menus that explain how
to use commands.  For example, type
^G

├────▼──1▼────▼───2▼────▼───3▼────▼──4▼────▼───5▼────▼───6▼────▼───┤
the Opening Menu and give the name of the document needing a changed
format.  You can then respond to the series of questions used to
initially create the format.  This method affects the entire document.

WordStar 2000 also lets you fine tune the format while working on a
document.  The format commands you give within the document override
the choices you made in the document format.  You can control format
├────▼──1▼────▼───2▼────▼───3▼────▼──4▼────▼───5▼────▼───6▼────▼───┤
WordStar 2000 offers a wide array of special print features.  The
commands are easily inserted into the document as you type or added
later while editing.  Although WordStar 2000 offers the features, the
printer determines which of the features can actually be printed.  Not
all printers are capable of producing all of the print features.

The special print features are found on the Print Enhancements Menu.
```

Fig. 4-11/WordStar 2000 screen with three windows.

second window in the middle of the screen.

**Moving Blocks Between Windows**—You can mark a block of text in one window, then move or copy it to another window. Open the windows and mark the desired block. Then move the cursor to another window with ^CW or Shift-F3 and position it where the marked block is to appear when moved or copied. Give the block move command— ^BM or F10—or block copy command— ^BC or Shift-F10.

You can have only one set of block markers set at any one time. For example, if a block is marked in the first window, marking a block in the second window unmarks the block in the first window.

**Closing a Window**—You close a window by saving it with the Quit and Save command, ^QS or Alt-1, or the Quit and Abandon command, ^QA or Alt-2. If you open two windows in the same document, keep in mind that you can save the edits in only one window. Use the second window in a document only for viewing or for marking text that will be transferred to another window.

## SPELLING CHECK OF A DOCUMENT

WordStar 2000 uses CorrectStar, a built-in dictionary with nearly 75,000 words, for checking the spelling of your documents. In addition, you can create personal dictionaries, very useful for storing specialized trade, legal, scientific or medical terms that are not part of CorrectStar's more general vocabulary.

To initiate the spelling check of a document, type ^OS for Option Spelling check. You then see the Spelling Correction Menu which gives your four choices:

1) W to check the spelling of one Word.
2) P to check the spelling of the Paragraph.
3) R to check the spelling of the Rest of the document.
4) S to Select a dictionary.

Type the letter of your choice. If you are using a computer with two disk drives, you will be prompted to remove the WordStar 2000 program disk from Drive A and insert the Dictionary disk. If the dictionary is installed on a hard disk, you will not need to switch disks.

Three of the above options also have short-cut commands:

1) Alt-5 to check the spelling of one word.
2) Alt-6 to check the spelling of the paragraph.
3) Alt-7 to check the spelling of the rest of the document.

With each of the commands, the position of the cursor identifies where the spelling is to begin. WordStar 2000 will check the spelling of the word or the entire paragraph, regardless of the cursor's position. It can be at the beginning, or anywhere within the word or paragraph. CorrectStar looks backward to find the beginning of the word or paragraph. When checking the rest of the document, CorrectStar begins at the point of the cursor and continues to the end of the document.

**Correcting a Word**—When CorrectStar locates a *suspect word,* one not found in its dictionary, it will suggest other possible spellings. You can select another word suggested by CorrectStar to replace the misspelled word or you can type the correction from the keyboard.

After you have checked the spelling of a document, WordStar 2000 will prompt you to remove the Dictionary disk and insert the WordStar 2000 program disk. Be sure to give one of the save commands to store the changed document on disk.

# Basics Of Page 5 Formatting

In Chapter 3 you learned about one of the primary ways to format WordStar 2000 documents—using stored formats. You remember that you can create and store formats, then use them repeatedly for documents you create. The format given to a document can be changed in one of two ways.

1) The first method was described in Chapter 3. You type F on the Opening Menu and give the name of the document needing a changed format. You can then respond to the series of questions used to initially create the format. This method affects the entire document.

2) WordStar 2000 also lets you fine-tune the format while working on a document. The format commands you give within the document override the choices you made in the document format. You can control format features like line spacing, centering, tabs, margins and page breaks within a document. Let's look at these format features one at a time to become familiar with the commands.

## LINE SPACING

The stored format you created for your WORKTEXT document sets line spacing at 6.00, single spacing. However, once you begin typing you may decide that you prefer to print the document double-spaced.

Type the line spacing command, ^PH for Print Height, at the beginning of the document. When the submenu appears, move the highlight to 3.00 and press Return. With the cursor at the beginning of the document when you type the command, the entire document will print double-spaced unless you later give the

^PH command again. If the cursor is located somewhere other than at the beginning of the document, double spacing will take effect at the point of the cursor. The command given in the document overrides the single spacing command in the stored format.

**Option Display On**—WordStar 2000 hides the code [LINE HEIGHT 3.00 LPI] in the document at the cursor point when the command is given. You can see the codes WordStar 2000 hides in your document by typing ^OD to turn on the Option Display. A shortcut for the command is pressing Shift-F1.

Give the same command again to hide the codes. To delete a displayed command code that is alone on a line, put the cursor on it and type ^RE to Remove Entire line or press Shift-F6, the same commands you would use to delete any other line of text. Commands surrounded by text can be removed using the character or word-delete commands.

## CHANGING MARGINS AND TABS

Unless you make a change while creating a format, the left margin is set at 1 and the right margin is 65, with tabs set every five spaces. Perhaps you noticed that only the right margin can be changed when defining a format and that tabs set while creating the format are set at equal intervals. However, both margins and tabs are easily changed when working on a document.

Unlike its older sibling, WordStar 2000 stores the settings on Ruler Lines hidden inside the document. This means that WordStar 2000 will remember from one session to the next how you want the Ruler Line set up, eliminating the need to reset the margins and tabs each time you work on the document. The Ruler Line is inserted into the document at the cursor position and affects all of the text that follows until another Ruler Line makes further changes. Like the line-spacing command, the Ruler Line is hidden in the text but can be displayed with the ^OD command. The Ruler Line at the top of the screen changes whenever the cursor crosses the hidden Ruler Line.

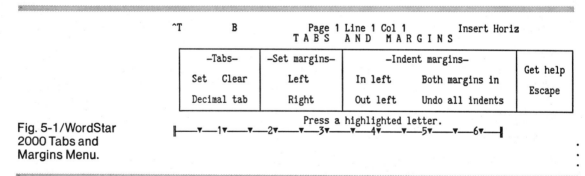

Fig. 5-1/WordStar 2000 Tabs and Margins Menu.

**Changing Margins**—Margins are set using the Tabs and Margins Menu shown in Figure 5-1. To see the menu on the screen, type ^T. Press L to set the Left margin and R to set the Right margin. A shortcut is to press F7 to set the left margin and Shift-F7 to set the right margin.

After you give either set of commands, WordStar 2000 asks

`Left Margin in what column?`

or

`Right Margin in what column?`

Type the number of the column where you want the margin set and press Return. The number WordStar 2000 supplies is the position of the cursor at the time you typed the ^TL or ^TR command. To accept that column number for the new margin setting, simply press Return.

When the margins are changed, WordStar 2000 inserts a Ruler Line into the document. The position of the right margin can be from 10 to 240 and must be at least 10 spaces from the left margin.

**Changing Tabs** — Tabs are also set and cleared using the Tabs and Margins Menu. Type ^TS for Tab Set or ^TC for Tab Clear. Again, you can use the Function keys for giving these commands: Press F8 to set a tab and Shift-F8 to clear a tab. With either set of commands WordStar 2000 asks

`Set tab in what column?`

or

`Clear tab in what column? (A for ALL)`

Type the number of the column where the tab is to be set or cleared and press Return. To clear all of the tabs, type A when WordStar 2000 asks which tab to clear and press Return. Again, the number WordStar 2000 provides is the cursor's position at the time you gave the command.

When the tabs change in a document, WordStar 2000 inserts a hidden Ruler Line.

## CENTERING TEXT

After you type a line, WordStar 2000 centers it with ^OC for Option Center, a command unchanged from WordStar. This command also has a shortcut, Shift-F2. You will see the text move on the screen to the centered position, where it will print.

When you give the center command, WordStar 2000 inserts the code [CENTER] into the text. A marked line of text recenters itself when the margins change, making it unnecessary to give the command more than once on the same line of text.

## CONTROLLING PAGE BREAKS

There are times when you need to be able to control the place WordStar 2000 begins a new page. For example, your document may include a 15-line table and you want to be sure all 15 lines *always* print on the same page. Or, your document is divided into two or more sections requiring each section to begin a new page. You must be able to give WordStar 2000 a command so new pages will begin only at ''approved'' places.

For the first example, you can insert a conditional page-break command to keep the 15 lines of the table on the same page. With the cursor at the beginning of the table, type ^OK for Options Keep lines together. WordStar 2000 prompts

`How many lines to keep together?`

asking you to type a number. In this case, type

`15`

and press Return. WordStar 2000 will insert a page break at the place the command was given *on the condition that* fewer than 15 lines remain on the page. This would cause the entire table to print on the next page.

If there are 15 or more lines left on the current page, the table prints within the document without beginning a new page. The code WordStar 2000 inserts is `[KEEP NEXT 15 LINES TOGETHER]`, the number matching the number you typed earlier.

You can also give WordStar 2000 a new page command that requires a new page to begin at the point of the cursor regardless of the number of lines remaining on the page. You would use this, for example, to begin a new section within a document. To do this, move the cursor to the point a new page must always begin and type ^OP for Option Page. You will immediately see the code `[PAGE]` on the screen followed by a line of dashes marking the page break. You can delete the command with the line-delete command, Shift-F6 or ^RE.

## AUTOMATIC HYPHENATION

When creating the WORKTEXT.FRM format using the series of questions in chapter 3, you answered Y to the question `Automatic Hyphenation?` This response permits WordStar 2000 to automatically hyphenate words as you type. The hyphens WordStar 2000 inserts are *soft* or *conditional* hyphens—they print only when actually used to divide a word at the end of a line. Only the hyphens you see on the screen will print.

You can further control word hyphenation by inserting conditional hyphens as you type. With the cursor marking the place for the conditional hyphen, type ^O-. This is the letter O, not zero, followed by a hyphen. To have this command work correctly, depress the Ctrl key only while typing the O, and release it before pressing the Hyphen key.

Turning the display on with ^OD reveals the code `[HYPHEN]` marking the conditional hyphen. To prevent a word from being hyphenated, type the ^O- command in front of the word.

## PAGE NUMBERING

Another decision you made while designing a format was whether pages will be printed with page numbers and if so, where on the page they appear: centered, left, right, or alternating left and right.

Unless otherwise specified, WordStar 2000 begins sequential numbering with 1. You can reset the page number at any time when you are working in a

document by typing ^OA for Option Assign page number.
    WordStar 2000 asks

Page number to assign?

Type the new desired page number. The page number on the Status Line remains unaffected, although the printed number reflects this command.

## HEADERS AND FOOTERS

There are times when you want one or more lines of text to print at the top or bottom of each printed page. Text printing at the top of the page is called a *header,* and text at the bottom of the page is called a *footer.* Headers and footers are useful for identifying the name, date, document title, or author on each page of a printed document. Headers and footers can also include the page number.

To define the text for a header, type the ^OH command. Type ^OF to type the footer text. In response to either command, WordStar 2000 prompts for the placement of the header or footer B, O, or E—for Both odd and even pages, for just Odd pages, or for just Even pages respectively.

Type the letter of your choice to set the frequency of the header or footer. WordStar 2000 provides the [HEADER] and [FOOTER] tags on the screen so you can type the text

[HEADER]
Life at Mount Vernon
[HEADER]

or

[FOOTER]
rev. November 16, 1985
[FOOTER]

**Page Numbers**—To include the page number in the header or footer, move the cursor to the space (column) where it is to print and type

&%PAGE&

For example, to print the page number at the right margin in the header above, this is what you will see on the screen:

[HEADER]
Life at Mount Vernon                                      &%PAGE&
[HEADER]

**Changing Headers and Footers**—Once you have defined headers or footers, they will print through the rest of the document. However, if you want to change the text in the header or footer, give the ^OH or ^OF command at the top of the page where the change is to begin. WordStar 2000 again provides tags. Type the new header or footer.

To omit the page number, give the ^OH or ^OF command at the place the change is to begin, and type the text without the page number code.

To begin numbering pages using the header or footer, give the appropriate command, and retype the text including &%PAGE&. To discontinue the header or footer entirely, give the ^OH or ^OF command, leaving the space between the tags blank.

WordStar 2000 allows you to define up to two different headers and two different footers. This means that you can print both a header and a footer on the same page. At the same time, you can specify one header that prints on odd-numbered pages and a different header for even-numbered pages. The same applies to footers.

During printing, one blank line is inserted to separate a header or footer from the rest of the text. If you want more space, include one or more blank lines between the tags—after the header text, or before the footer text.

**Formatting**—The format of headers and footers can be different than the rest of the document. For example, multiple lines of a header or footer can be single-spaced while the rest of the document prints double-spaced. footer can also have a Ruler Line with margins and tabs differing fr text.

Be aware that using headers and footers on pages reduces the nu available for text on the page. The top and bottom margins establis document format are respected, but the headers and footers borrow example, let's say your document is printed double-spaced with a o and a one-line footer on each page separated from the text by one b page will print with two fewer lines of text than it would if the head were omitted.

Headers and footers can each print multiple lines of text. The le is that the sum of the lines in the header and footer cannot exceed t and must leave room for at least one line of text.

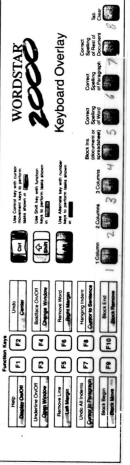

# *Special Print* 6
# *Characteristics*
# *& Printing*

WordStar 2000 offers a wide array of special print features. The commands are easy to insert into the document as you type. Or, you can add them later while editing. Although WordStar 2000 offers the features, the printer determines which features can actually be printed. Not all printers are capable of producing all print features.

The special print features are found on the Print Enhancements Menu. You can see the first of the two screens by typing

^P

while working on a document. Now press the Spacebar to see the second screen. They are shown in Figure 6-1.

## UNDERLINING

To underline a section of text, type ^PU for Print Underline or Shift-F4 at the beginning and end of the section. Notice that this command needs to be given in pairs—you turn the underline on and turn it off. When you type the command, WordStar 2000 inserts the code [U] at the cursor's position each time the command is given. (You can see the code by turning the display on with ^OD.)

Text marked with the underline command may be displayed on your monitor with the underline, or the section will be highlighted. During installation you can assign a color to identify underlined text on a color monitor.

WordStar 2000 is capable of printing either solid underlines, which appear below both words and the spaces between words, or broken underlines, which print below characters only, not spaces.

41

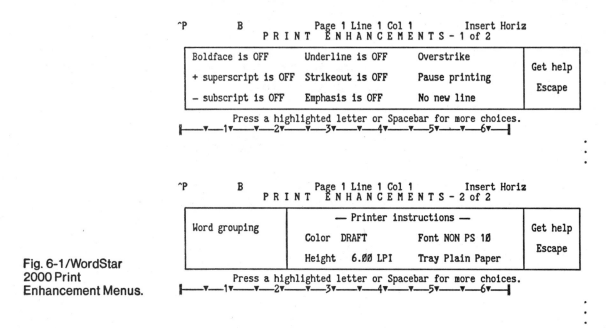

**Fig. 6-1/WordStar 2000 Print Enhancement Menus.**

You determine the kind of underline that will print when designing the document's format. WordStar 2000 asks

`Underline between underlined words? (Y/N) Y`

## BOLDFACE AND EMPHASIS

With most printers, both boldface and emphasis print cause text to be printed darker. In both cases the printer strikes each character more than once. Type ^PB for Print Bold or press F4. Type ^PE for Print Emphasis.

Like the underline command, boldface and emphasis print commands need to be given in pairs, once at the beginning of the section and once at the end. Text marked with the bold or emphasis commands will be displayed in a brighter color on most screens. The installation process allows you to assign different colors to the marked sections for display on a color monitor.

## COLOR AND QUALITY PRINTING

WordStar 2000 will print text using your printer's color capabilities. When you type ^PC for Print Color, the printer's color choices are listed. You select one by moving the computer screen's highlight bar with the Arrow keys to the desired color and pressing Return.

**Quality Printing**—Some printers incapable of printing in color use this command to let you choose print styles. For example, a dot matrix printer may offer choices called *quality* or *italic* in addition to its normal typestyle.

The *quality* selection uses the printer's correspondence or letter-quality emulation. The choices you see on your screen depend on the printer selected during the installation of WordStar 2000.

## SUPERSCRIPTS AND SUBSCRIPTS

A *superscript* is one or more characters that print raised above the normal line of text. For example, a footnote reference is frequently printed as a superscript. A *subscript* prints lowered below the normal print line. Both superscripts and subscripts are useful for chemical or mathematical formulas and notations. Here are some examples of superscripts and subscripts:

```
The desert Southwest's most precious natural resource is
water, H₂O.
```

```
The research of Clement Arbinger in 1984 listed others as
well.¹
```

To mark a superscript, type ^P+. Use either the plus key on the upper row of the keyboard or the one on the keypad. Then type the one or more characters that will be the superscript and repeat the ^P+ command. WordStar 2000 inserts the code [+]. Follow the same procedure for a subscript, except that you should type ^P-, using the Hyphen or Minus keys. WordStar 2000 inserts the code [-]. Keep in mind that both commands must be given in pairs, "bracketing" the superscript or subscript.

Some printers are incapable of printing superscripts and subscripts in their intended positions. Some printers leave them on the normal printing line, or raise and lower them by a whole line rather than a fraction of a line. You will also find that some printers are unable to combine another print feature such as boldface or emphasis with a superscripted or subscripted character.

## OVERPRINTING TEXT

WordStar 2000 has three commands for overprinting text. You can print one character on another or overprint one line of text with another.

**Overstrike**—First, you can overstrike one character with another character. You might do this, for example, to create some characters during printing that your keyboard doesn't have or to add diacritical marks to non-English words. The Print Overstrike command, ^PO, is one of the few special print commands that is *not* given in pairs. It is typed once and affects the characters that immediately precede and follow it.

Let's say that you want to type the simple mathematical statement A≠B. To do this, type

```
A=^PO/B
```

The printer will print the equal sign then the slash before moving to print the next character. Here are more characters you can create by overprinting

$$\leq \qquad \geq \qquad \pm \qquad ¢ \qquad \delta \qquad \tilde{n} \qquad \boxtimes \qquad \hat{e}$$

You can print more than two characters at the same spot simply by giving the overstrike command again.

You can combine other print commands like the superscript with the overstrike. For example, you might see that the tilde needs to be raised higher when printed over the n. To do this, add the superscript command to the tilde by typing

n^PO^P+^P+

but all you will see on the screen is

n~

**Strikeout**—The second way to overprint text is to use WordStar 2000's *Strikeout* command. Type ^PS for Print Strikeout at each end of the text that will be overprinted with hyphens. WordStar 2000 inserts the code [S].

This command could be useful for marking text that you feel could be deleted from a document but that should be printed awaiting another reader's approval.

**Line Overprinting**—The third command available to you prints one entire line over another. To do this, type the first line of text. Rather than pressing Return at the end of the line, type ^PN for Print No new line. WordStar 2000 inserts a hyphen at the right edge of the screen while the cursor moves to the next line. Now type the second line of text.

You could use this command, for example, to overprint a line with Xs or slashes rather than the hyphens offered by the Strikeout command. Let's say you want to overprint a line of text with slashes. First, type the line of text and then the proper command:

Mount Vernon is in Virginia.^PN

and press Return. Now type the backslash 28 times, once for each character and space in the sentence. When you print, the printed lines look like this:

M̸ø̸ú̸n̸t̸/V̸é̸r̸ñ̸ø̸n̸/ı̸s̸/ı̸ñ̸/V̸ı̸r̸g̸ı̸ñ̸ı̸á̸

If your printer is incapable of understanding the boldface command, you can produce boldface by using this command to print a line of text *twice* before moving to the next line. Or, if the boldface cannot be combined with another command such as the underline, print the line boldface and overprint it with the underline.

## SELECTING TYPE STYLES

The printer-definition file transferred to the WordStar 2000 disk during installation includes information about the sizes and styles of characters the selected printer can print. When you type ^PF for Print Font, you see a display of the installed printer's capabilities. WordStar 2000 asks

Font to use?

One selection, the default or the current setting in the document, is highlighted. Move the screen's highlight bar with the Arrow keys to the desired choice and press Return. Remember that the cursor's position at the time the command is given marks the place the font will change.

Depending on the printer you are using, you may see a choice like NON PS

10, meaning non-proportionally spaced characters printed 10 pitch (10 characters per inch). You will recall that proportional spacing allocates space to characters depending on their sizes, giving more to *m* than to *i,* for example. Other pitch choices may be listed, including 5, 8.5, 12, 15 or 20. You might see font or style names along with the pitch, such as *Courier 10* or *Helvetica 12.*

When you give the font command, WordStar 2000 inserts a code in the document stating the change — [NON PS 17] for example.

## OTHER PRINTING FEATURES

Remember that WordStar 2000 itself offers many special printing features, but the limiting factor is your printer's ability to do them.

**Printer Pause** — When you are using a printer with a removable print head or font cartridge, you must be able to stop the printer at a specified place in the document to change the font. You change the font by actually changing the printwheel or cartridge. Type ^PP for Print Pause at the point in the text that the printer is to stop.

For example, to print one paragraph using an italic print head, type the ^PP command at the beginning and the end of the paragraph. The first command stops the printer so you can install the italic printwheel or cartridge. The second command stops the printer so you can change back to the regular font.

**Controlling Word Breaks** — WordStar 2000 also lets you mark words that must always be printed on the same line. This helps you avoid undesirable word breaks like those shown in this example:

```
We are announcing the upcoming reunion for local veterans of WW
II who served as radio operators. Amateur and shortwave radio
has grown into a hobby for many of us.
```

For example, to fix the bad break in WW II you would type ^PW for Print Word grouping in the space between WW and II rather than pressing the Spacebar. WordStar 2000 inserts the code [W] and welds the two words together, treating them as one. This is helpful to prevent the separation of a person's name, a phone number, and other words that are more meaningful when kept together.

**Paper Trays** — If your printer is equipped with multiple paper trays, you can instruct WordStar 2000 regarding paper choice. When you type ^PT for Paper Tray, WordStar 2000 asks

```
Paper tray to use?
```

Your choices are Letterhead and Plain Paper. Move the highlight bar to the desired choice and press Return. You would use this, for example, to print the first page of a letter using your stationery and print successive pages on plain paper.

## PRINTING A DOCUMENT

Printing is a very important aspect of word processing, with WordStar 2000 letting you put on paper everything you have typed at the keyboard. It is after printing that you really see the formats and special touches you added to your document—headers and footers, justification, superscripts and subscripts, and more.

When you are at the Opening Menu, you simply type P to Print a file. WordStar 2000 then asks for the name of the file to print. Type the filename or move the highlight bar to the document of your choice and press Return.

Another way to give WordStar 2000 the command to print is to type the quit and print command, ^QP or Alt-4, when you are working on the document you wish to print. WordStar 2000 saves the document and proceeds to a decisions screen, which you see following either print command.

Following are the questions WordStar 2000 asks. Each requires a response. To accept all of the default answers type ^Q and press Return when the printer is ready.

**Begin printing on what page?**—The default is 1. To begin with a different page, type the number and press Return.

**Stop printing after what page? (L for LAST)**—The default is L, the Last page of the document. To stop printing after another page, type the number and press Return.

**Print how many copies?**—Default is 1. To type two or more copies, type a number between 1 and 1000 and press Return.

**Pause between pages for paper change? (Y/N)**—Default is N. Type Y and press Return if you need to insert a new sheet of paper for each page. The printer will stop during printing until you give the "resume" command.

**Obey page formatting commands? (Y/N)**—Default is Y. This means that WordStar 2000 will act on the format codes in the document. If you type N and press Return, all of the codes like [B] for boldface or [U] for underline will literally print rather than be used for formatting the document.

**Print and continue working? (Y/N)**—Default is N. Type Y and press Return to edit another document while this one prints. When printing begins, you will see the Opening Menu.

**Send document to Printer or ASCII Disk file? (P/D)**—Default is P for Printer. Type D and press Return to have WordStar 2000 print the document to a disk file. You will be prompted to provide the name for the disk file. Use this option to create an ASCII file, which is stripped of the command codes and can be read by many other word processors. You would also use this to ready a document for telecommunications.

## HOW TO INTERRUPT PRINTING

Once printing has begun you may want to stop it temporarily. A customer may demand your attention, the phone may ring, or you spot an error that needs to be corrected. Type P to stop the printer. If you are editing another document and need to stop the printer, type ^QP.

After either command, WordStar 2000 asks

```
Printing is interrupted:
Continue or Abandon? (C/A) C
```

When you are ready to resume printing, press Return because the C for Continue is the default. Type A to Abandon printing. In this case, printing is cancelled and the Opening Menu reappears on the screen. If you were editing another document, it remains on the screen.

This concludes Part I of the book. It gave you an overview of the commands and capabilities of WordStar 2000. The application projects in Part II allow you to become more familiar with these commands.

# Part II
# Applications
# Of WordStar 2000

Welcome to Part II, your guide to exploring the power of WordStar 2000. With your basic understanding of how WordStar 2000 works, you are well on your way to mastery! Although this won't happen instantly, you will acquire proficiency when you see how commands actually affect documents. You need examples and practice. That is the purpose of Part II.

Each chapter in Part II covers the preparation of a different document, illustrating the application of WordStar 2000 features for the document's special needs.

You will learn ways of typing correspondence, one of the most frequent tasks of WordStar 2000 users. You will look at preparing outlines and research papers, using footnotes and math, working with columns and repetitious documents, and merge printing. These examples will lead you to proficiency with WordStar 2000, making it create, format and print documents as you want them.

As you read Part I, you may have asked "But can WordStar 2000 do this?" or "Could I do this in my document an easy way?" or "Will I really ever want to use this command?"

You are about to find the answers to questions like these. You just might discover uses for nearly all of WordStar 2000's array of commands!

# *Typing Letters & Memos* 7

Whether you use WordStar 2000 at home, in an office, or at school, you will type correspondence frequently. You type a letter for your boss or a memo requesting a raise. You write to Uncle Joe for his birthday or compose a quick thank-you note to Sarah for helping you with a car problem. You prepare a cover letter to accompany your book proposal to the publisher, your job application for that long-awaited career opportunity, and your request to the utility company for the promised deposit refund.

How can you do these things quickly and easily? Let's look at how WordStar 2000 performs each of these kinds of tasks.

## LETTER FORMAT

Remember that when you create a document, you set up or select a stored format for it. Because you are likely to do a significant amount of correspondence, a format for letters and perhaps another for memos will be useful. Then each time you type a letter or memo, you simply select the desired file to format your document.

You may be able to set up one format that will meet most of your correspondence needs. However, if some changes are necessary, that's easy too.

**LETTER.FRM**—You are now ready to design a format named *LETTER.FRM* to be used for the first example of this chapter. Remember from Part I what you need to do: From the Opening Menu, press F to select Format design. Name this format:

`LETTER.FRM`

Remember that the extension FRM on the filename lets WordStar 2000 identify this as a format file.

WordStar 2000 then asks the series of questions for setting up the format. Design your format as follows, using the Arrow keys to move the highlight bar to the desired choice or type the necessary letter or number and press Return. Press Return for the default selection. When it is complete, save it.

Font: 10 characters per inch
Line height (spacing): 6.00
Top margin: 6
Bottom margin: 6
Right margin: 60
Tab set interval: 5
Lines per page: 66
Even page offset: 12
Odd page offset: 12
Justified/Ragged: R
Automatic hyphenation: Y
Form feeds: Y or N depends on the printer's requirements
Underline between words: Y
Display page breaks: Y
Page Numbers: N

Take a moment to look over the choices you made for the letter format. Although several of these format items may change in other kinds of documents, letters are almost always single-spaced (line height 6.00) and are printed without page numbers at the bottom of the page. If page numbers are used for multiple-page letters, they usually appear at the top of the page. This is covered a bit later in this chapter.

The format you just designed is only one of many possible combinations of features for well-designed correspondence. Matters of margins, justification, and hyphenation are influenced by personal preference. Some people appreciate the neatness of right-justified lines. Others prefer leaving the right margin ragged. In some situations, you may want to avoid hyphenation to prevent possible misinterpretation of the text.

## ONE-PAGE BUSINESS LETTER

When the format is created and stored, you see the Opening Menu on the screen. You're ready to start work on a letter. Remember to change the drive or directory now with option D if you need to.

To begin work on a new document, type

E

and name the document

SAMUELS.THX

This is code for an example thank-you letter to one of your clients named Samuels who lets your travel agency make all of her travel arrangements.

**Typing the Letter**—Type the letter as you see it here. Remember to let WordStar 2000 wrap words to a new line as you type the paragraphs of the letter.

```
May 16, 1985


Harriet Samuels
1221 West Alameda
Chicago, IL 60660
Dear Harriet:
It was our pleasure to make travel arrangements for your
visit to Mazatlan last month. I trust that you and your
traveling companions had a delightful vacation in the sun.
As you know, WELLINGTON TRAVEL is coordinating a 9-day "by
land and sea" cruise and rail trip to Alaska in July, a 6-
day tour of the Hawaiian Islands in November, and a 15-day
Adventure to Europe in June, 1986. You will find further
information about each of these enclosed.
Thank you for letting WELLINGTON TRAVEL serve you. Should
you have any questions about these tours, please don't
hesitate to call me at the number printed on the brochure.
Sincerely,


Sidney Russet
Tour Coordinator
WELLINGTON TRAVEL
Enclosures
```

When the letter is typed, you see it on the screen as it will later print.
**Making Revisions**—It is not unusual to make changes in a letter after it is written for the first time. You may see that some facts were not correct or that you could have said things in a better way. You may also want to rearrange the order of text in your document.

Following is a copy of the letter you just typed with editing changes marked on it. Let's go through the steps to make the indicated changes. Some words need to be removed and others inserted. You will also use the block feature to switch the order of the first two paragraphs. Survey the changes you will make, then follow the steps for making the changes that follow the letter.

May 16, 1985

Harriet Samuels
1221 West Alameda — *spell out*
Chicago, IL 60660
Dear Harriet:

*I'm confident you will be interested in our new schedule.*

It was our pleasure to make travel arrangements for your visit to Mazatlan ~~last month~~. *earlier this year.* I trust that you and your traveling companions had a delightful vacation in the sun.

~~As you know,~~ WELLINGTON TRAVEL is coordinating a 9-day "by land and sea" cruise and rail trip to Alaska in July, a 6-day tour of the Hawaiian Islands in November, and a 15-day Adventure to Europe in June, 1986. ~~You will find further information about each of these enclosed.~~ *The descriptive brochures you requested are enclosed.*

Thank you for letting WELLINGTON TRAVEL serve you. Should you have any questions about these tours, please don't hesitate to call me at the number printed on the brochure.

Sincerely,

~~Sidney Russet~~ *your name*
Tour Coordinator
WELLINGTON TRAVEL

Enclosures

**Inside Address** — Using the cursor-movement diamond keys or the Arrow keys on the keypad, move the cursor to the *L* of *IL* and press the *Del* key to remove the *L*. Now type

```
llinois
```

The letters you type should appear on the screen, pushing the zip code to the right. If this doesn't happen, be sure the Status Line at the top of the screen says `Insert`. If you see `Over`, press the Ins key once. If you already typed over some of the letters you wanted to keep, you need to retype them.

**First Paragraph** — Move the cursor to the word *last* in the first sentence of the first paragraph. You will delete the words *last month* and replace them with the words *earlier this year.* You can do this in one of several ways. Three possible methods are described here to illustrate WordStar 2000's versatility:

1) Delete the words *last month* by giving the Remove Word command twice. Do it by pressing F6 twice or type

```
^RW^RW
```

Now type the words

```
earlier this year.
```

Remember to type the period because it was removed with the second Remove Word command.

2) Delete the words *last month* using the Remove To a character command, ^RT. With the cursor positioned on the *l* of *last,* type

`^RT`

When WordStar 2000 prompts

`Remove from cursor to what character?`

type a period. The words *last month* are removed, but the period stays in place. After making certain that the word `Insert` appears on the Status line at the top of the screen, type

`earlier this year`

3) This method takes advantage of the choice you have to type over text as a way to remove it. Again, with the cursor on the *l* of *last,* press the Ins key once so the word `Over` appears on the top line of the screen. Now type the first 10 characters of the new words

`earlier th`

and you will see that the previous text has disappeared. But because the text you are putting in is longer than the text you are typing over, you must now press the Ins key again so the remaining characters can be inserted. Press Ins and resume typing

`is year`

The final change to this paragraph is the addition of an entire sentence at the end. Position the cursor after the period that now ends the final sentence. Press the Spacebar twice to insert blank spaces. Type the new sentence

`I'm confident you will be interested in our new schedule.`

**Second Paragraph**—The first three words of the second paragraph need to be removed. Position the cursor at the beginning of the first line. Now give the Remove Word command three times. Press F6 three times or type

`^RW^RW^RW`

The three words are removed and WordStar 2000 automatically closes the gap by shifting the entire line to the left. Notice that the remaining lines of the paragraph also shift.

Also, the entire last sentence of the paragraph needs to be deleted and a new sentence typed in its place. Again, there are several ways you can do this:

1) The easiest way to remove the existing sentence is to use WordStar 2000's Remove Sentence command, ^RS. Put the cursor anywhere in the sentence—the beginning, the end, or anywhere between—and type

`^RS`

The entire sentence disappears. Press the Spacebar if necessary to insert blank spaces, then type the new sentence

`The descriptive brochures you requested are enclosed.`

    2) Another way to change the last sentence of the paragraph is simply to type the new sentence over the old one. Press Ins once so the word `Over` appears on the Status Line. Now type

`The descriptive brochures you requested are enclosed.`

The new sentence you typed is shorter than the old one. You can quickly remove the leftover fragment by typing

`^RR`

for the Remove Right command. Everything from the cursor to the right end of the line is deleted.

    Other ways of deleting the fragment are pressing the Spacebar—when `Over` appears on the Status Line; pressing the Del key; or giving the Remove Word command, `^RW` or F6, until the extra characters are gone.

**Moving Paragraphs**—Now you need to reverse the order of the first two paragraphs. To do this, you must mark either of the paragraphs as a block, reposition the cursor, and give the Move Block command.

    It doesn't make any difference which paragraph you mark. However, because the cursor is already in the second paragraph, let's mark it. Move the cursor to the beginning of the paragraph, placing it on the *W* of *Wellington.* Give the Begin Block command by typing

`^BB`

or press F9. You should see

`<B>`

inserted at the point of the cursor.

    To mark the end of the block, move the cursor to the *T* of *Thank* that begins the third paragraph. Type

`^BE`

for Block End or press Shift-F9 [F10]. The entire marked block is highlighted. Placing the cursor on the first character of the next paragraph includes the blank line in the block. When this block is moved, it will be properly separated from the paragraph that follows it. The first character of the following paragraph, however, is not included in the marked block. WordStar 2000 inserts this command and others just to the left of the cursor.

    Now move the cursor to mark the block's new location. Put the cursor on the first character of the first paragraph, the *I* of *It.* Give the Block Move command by typing

`^BM`

or pressing F10. *Shift-F9* Watch the marked block appear at the new location. The first two paragraphs of the letter have exchanged places.

**Closing**—The final change is to put your name on the signature line in place of Sidney's. Use one of the Remove commands to take out *Sidney Russet,* or type your name over it. Look over your work and make sure it agrees with the edited letter on page 52.

**Saving the Letter**—Because you have made several changes to the letter, save the document before adding a few final touches. Type

^QC

to Quit and Continue or use the Alt-3 key combination to give the command. This command updates the document named SAMUELS.THX on the disk but leaves the document on the screen so you can continue working on it.

**Space for Letterhead**—The letter is nearly ready to print. You plan to use the Wellington Travel stationery which has the imprint preprinted at the top of the paper. This means you need to allow for extra space at the top of the page for the letterhead. There are two ways to do this. With either method, you need to know how much space needs to be allocated for the letterhead before the date line of the letter prints.

When you use your own letterhead, get out a ruler and measure the space in inches from the top of the paper to the place the first line of the letter can be reasonably printed. Leave a comfortable distance between the lowest part of the imprint and the first line of print. Let's assume that you measure your paper (imagining that it is letterhead for Wellington Travel) and determine that you need three inches at the top of the letter.

Now a quick math lesson: The top margin for LETTER.FRM, the format used for typing this letter, is set at six lines per inch. There are six lines of printing in one vertical inch on the printed page. If you now print the letter, six lines will be left blank and printing will begin on the seventh line from the top of the page—assuming that you align the top edge of the paper with the print head on the printer.

Printing will begin within the area reserved for the imprint. That's not what you want. You want three blank inches before printing begins. Therefore, 6 lines per inch times 3 inches equals 18 blank lines for proper printing.

1) One solution to the problem is to insert 18 blank lines at the beginning of the document. The current top margin setting supplies 6, so you need to put in 12 more blank lines.

Move the cursor to the *M* of *May* on the date line and press Return until the Status Line reports that the cursor is on line 13. This indicates that 12 blank lines were added to the six lines in the top margin that precede the date. When you print the letter, printing will begin below the company imprint.

2) The second solution involves changing the size of the top margin in the

format of the document. To use this method, save the letter by typing

```
^QS
```

or pressing *Alt-1*. When you see the Opening Menu on the screen, press

```
F
```

to select the Format Design option. When WordStar 2000 asks

```
Format or formatted document name?
```

type

```
SAMUELS.THX
```

and press Return. Continue to press Return to leave choices unchanged until you see the question

```
How many lines in the top margin?
```

The answer WordStar 2000 supplies is 6 because that's how the format is now designed. However, you want an 18-line margin, so type

```
18
```

and press Return. Continue to press Return to leave the other answers unchanged. When the sequence of questions is complete, type

```
S
```

to Save the changes. Now when the SAMUELS.THX letter is printed, 18 lines are automatically put into the top margin.

**Things to Remember**—Use only one of these methods, not both. If you combined the two methods, you would have 30 blank lines at the top of the page, 18 because the top margin is set at 18 lines plus 12 due to the blank lines inserted in method 1.

Keep in mind that if you write a letter to another of your clients using the LETTER.FRM format, the top margin remains at six lines. When the format of the SAMUELS.THX letter was changed to include an 18-line top margin, only that letter was affected. The LETTER.FRM format file is unchanged.

**Advantages and Disadvanages**—You may find that one of the methods works better for you than the other. Let's say that you add several more paragraphs to Harriet Samuels' letter so it becomes a two-page letter. If you changed the format of the document to require an 18-line top margin, the second page will also begin printing three inches down.

Because the second page doesn't have the company imprint, you don't need the large top margin. So you can see that changing the format may not be the best solution if you prepare letters longer than one page.

In this case, it would be better to manually insert the blank lines at the top of the first page so the second page will print at the desired place on the paper. More on that in the next section.

However, if your letters are generally one page long and you use imprinted paper, changing the stored format may be the easiest method. This makes

WordStar 2000 responsible for inserting the necessary blank lines at the top of the page, an easy thing for you to overlook.

**Let Key Glossaries Help**—To make letter writing easier, you can set up several keys, store them in a glossary, and recall them at will. If you were to type a quantity of letters for Wellington Travel, two sections of text could be stored and recalled to make your typing less repetitive. These are *WELLINGTON TRAVEL* and the letter's closing.

Let's go through the steps to put these two phrases into a Key Glossary. You can do this from either the Opening Menu by pressing

K

or while working on a document by typing

^KD

for Key Define. Choose the appropriate command, depending upon what you see on your screen now. If you changed the document format earlier, you will be at the Opening Menu. If you inserted blank lines to increase the size of the top margin, you are likely to still be in the document.

WordStar 2000 asks

Short form to define?

Type

WT

for *WELLINGTON TRAVEL.* Press Return and you see

Long form?

Then type

WELLINGTON TRAVEL

Use all caps because that's how your want WordStar 2000 to type it for you. When you type

^Q

to end the long form, WordStar 2000 offers the opportunity to define another short form. Type

closing

when WordStar 2000 asks you to define the short form. Then press Return. Now type the long form that WordStar 2000 will type for you, pressing Return after each line and to create the blank lines.

Sincerely,

--(your name)--
Tour Coordinator
WELLINGTON TRAVEL

Type

`^Q`

to end the long form. Notice that pressing Return doesn't end the text. It simply moves the cursor to a new line so you can continue typing.

When WordStar 2000 gives you the chance to type another short form, press Esc to terminate the defining process. When WordStar 2000 asks

`Should these changes be saved? (Y/N) N`

type

`Y`

to save them. Next you specify the key file in response to the prompt

`Key file to use?`

Type

`LETTERS.KEY`

and press Return. This name indicates that short and long forms you frequently use when typing letters are stored in this key file.

The next time you type a letter, you can recall these stored phrases. Select the key file named LETTERS.KEY by typing

`^KU`

highlighting LETTERS.KEY, and pressing Return. When you return to the document, type

`WT`

and press Esc when you want the words WELLINGTON TRAVEL to appear. At the end of the letter, type

`closing`

and press Esc to have WordStar 2000 supply the closing for you.

## MULTI-PAGE BUSINESS LETTER

The previous example showed you how easy it is to type, change, and format a one-page letter. When the letter is two or more pages, you may need to adjust the top margin and use headers and page numbers. Giving special attention to these details lets you produce professional-looking printed documents.

**Top Margin—**As already mentioned, the top margin is an important consideration when typing letters more than one page long. Usually, the first page is printed on company or personal letterhead. The second page and all succeeding pages print on plain paper with a top margin somewhat smaller than that of the first page.

You recall that there are at least two ways to change the top margin in a document—inserting blank lines at the top of the page or changing the document's format. When working with a document several pages in length with varying top margins, it is easiest to insert the blank lines to produce a larger top margin. This is because when the size of the top margin is changed in the format, it affects all pages of the document.

**Using Headers**—In a multi-paged letter, it is common to include the addressee's name, date, and page number at the top of the page. These may be printed on three lines at the left margin. For example:

```
Harriet Samuels
May 16, 1985
Page 2
```

Or it may be on one line across the top of the page, as in:

```
Harriet Samuels            -2-            May 16, 1985
```

You can have WordStar 2000 print one or more lines of text on each page automatically, with pages numbered sequentially. To see how this is done, you can add more text to the SAMUELS.THX document so it becomes two pages long. But before changing the letter, be sure the format of the document is as you want it.

If you changed the size of the top margin to 18 lines in the format of the document in the previous section, change it back to 6 lines. Remember that the best way to change the size of the top margin in a multi-page document is simply to insert blank lines at the top of the first page. If necessary, add or delete lines so the date line appears on line 13.

Because the paragraphs being added to the letter describe the scheduled tours, the first paragraph is no longer necessary. Delete it by putting the cursor anywhere in the paragraph and typing

```
^RP
```

for Remove Paragraph. Move the cursor to the first letter of the second of the remaining paragraphs. Press

```
^CI
```

twice to insert two blank lines, making room to begin typing the three additional paragraphs. Now type paragraphs two, three and four to make the SAMUELS.THX letter two pages long.

May 16, 1985

Harriet Samuels
1221 West Alameda
Chicago, Illinois 60660

Dear Harriet:

It was our pleasure to make travel arrangements for your visit to Mazatlan earlier this year. I trust that you and your traveling companions had a delightful vacation in the sun. I'm confident you will be interested in our new schedule.

First, we are planning a one-week computer literacy cruise in the Hawaiian Islands in April, 1986. Each day's itinerary includes several hours of hands-on time with the most popular business software. It will include lectures and training sessions with experts in word processing, electronic spreadsheets, databases, and business graphics software. In most cases, at least a portion of the cruise expenses are tax deductible.

For the thrill of historical adventure, you can spend three weeks with us in Israel, visiting several prominent archeological dig sites. This trip begins June 4, 1986. You will see Beersheba, Megiddo, ancient Jericho and excavation on the Temple Mount in Jerusalem. A three-day guided bus tour will also let you see other parts of this exciting country including an overnight stay at a kibbutz in Galilee. Other highlights of the tour include wading in the Mediterranean and Dead Seas, a boat ride on the Sea of Galilee, and a visit to the famous Church of the Nativity in Bethlehem.

Our special trip to Europe in 1986 commemorates the 301st birthdays of two of history's most significant musicians and composers—Johann Sebastian Bach and George Frederick Handel. The tour highlights famous castles, cathedrals and music schools in England, Germany, France, Switzerland, and Austria. You will hear concerts of Bach and Handel works performed on instruments of the period in the music rooms and cathedrals the composers had in mind during their writing. Plan to pick up many of your souvenirs directly from craftsmen in the countryside. We will also be visiting several of Europe's outstanding art museums. This tour leaves June 17.

Thank you for letting WELLINGTON TRAVEL serve you. Should you have any questions about these tours, please don't hesitate to call me at the number printed on the brochure.

Sincerely,

--(your name)--
Tour Coordinator
WELLINGTON TRAVEL
Enclosures

Now that the letter is revised, let's add the header. Move the cursor to the first character of the second page. Type

^OH

for Option Header. Before typing the text for the header, you must specify how frequently it will be printed. On the screen you will see

place this header on:

Both odd and even pages    Odd pages only    Even pages only

Type

B

to print the header on Both odd and even pages. Then WordStar 2000 displays

[HEADER]

[HEADER]

on the screen. You now type the text of the header just as it will print.

**Multi-Line Header—**Using the style that places the name, date and page on separate line, you type

Harriet Samuels
May 16, 1985
Page &%PAGE&

and press Return twice. The screen shows this

[HEADER]
Harriet Samuels
May 16, 1985
Page &%PAGE&

[HEADER]

The code &%PAGE& will be replaced by the actual page number during printing. Because you know that your letter is only two pages long, you could have typed

Page 2

instead of &%PAGE&. However, if the letter (or any other document) is longer than two pages, using the &%PAGE& code is the easiest way of handling page numbering in the header. The same applies to footers.

You may recall from Part I that the header (or footer) prints on the page separated by one automatic blank line from the rest of the text. You pressed Return twice after typing the text of the header. This means that there are two blank lines as part of the header, making a total of three blank lines separating the header from the text on the second page.

**One-Line Header**—If you prefer the one-line header with the same information, give the header command

^OH

Again type

B

to print the header on even and odd pages. When the header markers appear, add the text and press Return twice so your screen looks like this:

```
[HEADER]
Harriet Samuels          Page &%PAGE&          May 16, 1985

[HEADER]
```

**Printing**—Now print the letter to Harriet Samuels. You can save the letter and initiate the printing by typing

^QP

for Quit and Print or use Alt-4. Respond to the print questions. How did you do?

If printing does not proceed smoothly, check the document to be certain the header command appears before any text on the first line of the second page.

## INTEROFFICE MEMOS

When you type interoffice memos, you will use many of the same steps used in typing letters. You may want to set up a MEMO.FRM file to set up the format you will use for memos.

**Key Glossaries**—You can set up a key glossary to store the heading for the memo, for example

```
                    MEMORANDUM

TO:
FROM:     Sidney Russet, Tour Coordinator
SUBJECT:
DATE:
```

You can include special print characteristics like center, boldface, underline, and font changes in the key glossary.

To do this, define a key glossary by typing

`K`

at the Opening Menu or

`^KD`

from within a document. Name the short form *MEMO* and press Return. You can now define the long form. When WordStar 2000 displays

`Long form?`

You will type all of the text and commands that will be part of the memorandum heading. You recall that the long form can be up to seven lines long with a maximum of 80 characters per line. This example includes two special print features, centering and boldfacing.

To insert the commands, you must type the caret using the uppercase part of the 6 key (do not use the Ctrl Key) followed by the other letters normally typed to give the commands. For example, usually you give the command for boldface using `^PB` or F4. However, to include the boldface command in the long form, you will not use either of these commands.

Rather, you must literally type the characters—a caret, then P, then B. You will follow the same guidelines for the center command. Rather than typing `^OC` or Shift-F2, you will type the three characters—caret, then O, then C.

To include the tab in the long form, press the Tab Key. You will see `^I` on the screen representing the tab.

Type the long form text and press Return as follows:

`^OC^PBM E M O R A N D U M^PB`

and press Return twice. Then type

`^PBTO:^PB`

and press Return. Then type

`^PBFROM:^PB`

and press Tab twice, type your name, and press Return. Type

`^PBSUBJECT:^PB`

and press Return. Type

`^PBDATE:^PB`

and press Return. When the long form is complete, type

`^Q`

to end. When the screen displays the short-form prompt, press Esc because you don't want to define another short form now. Save the changes and assign this key to a glossary named *MEMO.KEY.*

**Using the Memo Heading**—When you begin work on a memo document, type

^KU

so you can identify which Key glossary you will use. Move the highlight bar to MEMO.KEY and press Return. To have WordStar 2000 supply the memo heading, put the cursor at the beginning of the document. Type

MEMO

and press Esc. WordStar 2000 types the entire memo heading on the screen for you! Now you can go back to add the addressee's name, the subject and the date.

## PERSONAL LETTER

The format you use for typing personal correspondence might be identical to that used for business correspondence. However, personal correspondence is often different because it is printed on non-standard paper.

Let's say that you can easily insert single sheets of paper into your printer and want to print on 6-1/2x8-inch paper. When paper size changes, you need to use a special format.

**Changing Format**—Before beginning the personal letter, create a format named *PERS-LTR.FRM* to identify it as the format for personal letters. Respond as follows to the format questions.

Font: 10
Line spacing: 6.00
Lines in top margin: 6
Lines in bottom margin: 6
Right margin: 55
Tab set interval: 5
Lines per page: 48
Even page offset: 5
Odd page offset: 5
Justified/Ragged: your choice
Automatic hyphenation: your choice
Form feeds: depends on your printer's requirements
Underline between words: your choice
Display page breaks: Y
Page numbers: N

**Setting Margins**—You can leave the top and bottom margins at the default setting of 6, but the right margin changes. The paper is 6-1/2 inches wide, allowing a maximum of 65 characters if pitch is 10 characters per inch. With the page offset of 5 and leaving approximately the same amount of space on the right edge of the paper, the right margin is set at 55.

If you decide to change the right margin while working on the document, you can do that easily by typing

`^TR`

followed by the column number and Return.

**Page Offset**—The page offset is smaller so printing begins closer to the left edge of the paper.

**Lines Per Page**—Your paper is now eight inches long for a total page length of 48 lines. This is calculated by multiplying the number of inches (8) by the number of lines per inch (6). Remember to change this number any time you use paper longer or shorter than the standard 11 inches (66 lines).

**Printing**—After giving the print command (P) on the Opening Menu, you can accept the default settings on the Print Decisions Screen with the exception of one. It's safe to assume that your personal stationery consists of loose sheets rather than continuous perforated paper. Therefore you need to ask WordStar 2000 to pause printing between pages so you can insert a new paper.

## TYPING THE ENVELOPE IN TYPEWRITER MODE

Let's say that you have now typed the business or personal letter or memo and have saved it on disk with the Quit and Save command, `^QS` or Alt-T. You're back at the Opening Menu. You can now quickly address the envelope for the letter using WordStar 2000's Typewriter Mode. Without naming a document and choosing a format, you can type and print text line by line. What you type, however, will not be saved on a disk.

At the Opening Menu type

`T`

to choose the Typewriter mode. The screen changes, and you can now type the text. Insert the envelope into the printer. Printing will take place at the print head, so roll the envelope to the position of the first line of the address. If you are using a business envelope, press the Spacebar until the Status Line at the top of the screen reports that the cursor is in column 40.

Type the first line

`Harriet Samuels`

and press Return. The first line of the address prints. Move the cursor to column 40 again, then type

`1221 West Alameda`

and press Return to print the second line. Again move the cursor to column 40 and continue by typing the third line

`Chicago, IL 60660`

and press Return to print this line. To return to the Opening Menu, type

`^Q`

or press Esc. The line is *buffered,* or held, in memory until you press Return. This gives you the opportunity to make corrections on the line before it is printed. Use cursor movement commands to move to the left and right on the line of text. When the line is letter perfect, press Return to print it. Once you have pressed Return, you cannot return to the line to make further changes.

Some printers allow you to turn the buffer off and on by typing

^B

When the buffer is off, what you type at the keyboard is immediately sent to the printer. This permits you to fill in preprinted forms by moving the print head to the exact spot where text is to print. If the printer itself has a buffer, the buffer feature in the Typewriter Mode cannot be turned off.

**Limitations**—Although typing in the Typewriter Mode is convenient, it also has some limitations. You can print only in the normal or default typestyle. Special print features like boldface and underline cannot be used. Because no margins are in effect, you cannot center text. The Tab key is disabled, so you must press the Spacebar to move the cursor. Also remember that whatever you type in the Typewriter Mode cannot be saved on the disk.

# *Generating* 8
# *Repetitious*
# *Documents*

WordStar 2000 makes creating repetitious or nearly identical documents quick and easy. You need only type the repetitious sections once, store them, and beckon them back when needed. The stored material is sometimes called *boilerplate text.* This chapter assumes that the volume of repetitious documents is relatively small, perhaps 10 to 20 per week. It is also assumed that the documents vary enough to require a human decision.

The particular information that makes each document unique cannot be put into a data file and inserted into the standard document at specified points. That's a job done by WordStar 2000's MailMerge, covered in a later chapter. You would use MailMerge, for example, for larger quantities of personalized, repetitious documents like a form letter going to all of your clients in Tennessee.

## TYPICAL REPETITIOUS DOCUMENTS

You probably won't search long before finding a half dozen examples of repetitious documents you could generate more easily than you are now doing. Examples include: letters of acceptance or denial for a club membership, real estate appraisal reports, offers to purchase, credit reports and other documents using a pool of standard paragraphs. The paragraphs are typed once, stored, and recalled on demand.

Other kinds of documents stay much the same except for "blanks" that need to be filled in to make each document unique. You may need to supply names, dates, businesses, or addresses. Rental or lease agreements, news releases, court documents, wills, job estimates and many other kinds of documents fit this category.

To produce these documents, you need only know where to fill in the appropriate information. You will use WordStar 2000's Locate feature to help you do this.

The methods of this chapter require the minimum amount of repetitious typing on your part. Let WordStar 2000's Block and Locate commands do the work while you collect the praise for generating many nice-looking documents in a short time!

## TECHNIQUES WITH STORED TEXT

To see how you can work with stored text to construct new documents, let's assume that you are sending personal letters from Wellington Travel to individuals inquiring about one of your tours. Your response to some of the letters is of a general nature, describing the highlights of the tour. Other letters acknowledge the receipt of the required deposit or remind the tour-goer to submit the deposit to guarantee the reservation. Some participants must be reminded to complete other forms, such as the medical release.

If you type the responses one at a time, you will soon discover that you must repeat the same material a lot. Instead, you can choose appropriate, pre-written paragraphs to build your letter, significantly reducing typing time.

**Typing Repetitious Paragraphs**—The general method is to type the repetitious paragraphs once, store each in a separate file on a disk, and then recall them to assemble a personalized letter.

Following are the paragraphs that meet most of your correspondence needs. Type these paragraphs in a document named *REPLIES,* using the LETTER.FRM format you set up in the previous chapter.

WELLINGTON TRAVEL's roster of tours for 1986 is our finest yet. Enclosed please find a picture brochure that describes each of our three major tours. To assure your reservation, submit the application form with the deposit required for the tour of your choice.

I'm sure you will enjoy the 7-day Computers At Sea literacy cruise in the Hawaiian Islands. You will fly from Los Angeles to Honolulu on April 17 and board the cruise ship the next morning. Each day's itinerary includes several hours of hands-on time under the tutelage of the country's foremost experts in word processing, electronic spreadsheets, databases, and business graphics programs. Refer to the enclosed brochure for IRS regulations regarding tax deductions for this type of training.

Archaeology in Israel, WELLINGTON TRAVEL's most popular tour, is being repeated in 1986. This historical adventure will take you to Israel for three weeks beginning June 4 where

you'll see excavation in progress at Beersheba and the
Temple Mount in Jerusalem. You'll learn about several ancient civilizations as you tour Megiddo, Jericho and Qumran.
Spend a night on a kibbutz in Galilee, wade in the Dead Sea,
take a boat ride on the Sea of Galilee, make a pilgrimage to
the famous Church of the Nativity in Bethlehem and more!

Music lovers will be thrilled with this year's tour to
Europe commemorating the 301st birthdays of two of history's
most significant musicians and composers-Johann Sebastian
Bach and George Frederick Handel. This tour departs June 17
to take you to famous castles, cathedrals, art museums, and
music schools in England, Germany, France, Switzerland, and
Austria. Imagine hearing the music of Bach and Handel performed with period instruments in the music rooms and
cathedrals the composers frequented!

This letter confirms your reservation for the Computers At
Sea cruise in the Hawaiian Islands beginning April 17, 1986.

The Archaeology in Israel Tour is filling fast. Although I
already have your reservation form, the reservation is not
confirmed until WELLINGTON TRAVEL receives the deposit.
You'll want to take care of this immediately so you don't
miss this trip of a lifetime.

This letter confirms your reservation for the Archeology in
Israel adventure tour departing June 4, 1986. If you have
not already done so, be sure to get your passport or make
certain the one you have is valid.

This letter confirms your reservation for the Music Lovers'
Tour of Europe departing June 17. If you have not already
done so, be sure to get your passport or make certain the
one you have is valid.

Due to the physical limitations or special medical needs you
specified on your reservation form, you need to complete the
enclosed medical release form. A portion of the form
requires your doctor's approval for participating in the
tour. Your reservation will be held by the deposit and will
be refunded to you if your physician denies travel approval.

Also let me remind you of our special offer. If you and
three of your friends register for the same tour and pay the
required deposit before October 15, 1985, each of you will
receive a 15% discount on the total tour price! Never
before has WELLINGTON TRAVEL made such a generous discount
offer.

```
Sincerely,

Sidney Russet
Tour Coordinator
WELLINGTON TRAVEL
```

After typing the paragraphs, save and print the file by typing

```
^QP
```

or pressing Alt-4. The printed list will be your reference for selecting paragraphs when writing letters.

After printing, number each paragraph on the paper, using the codes *T-1, T-2, T-3* and so on through *T-11*. The code *T* identifies these as *Tour* paragraphs.

**Storing Repetitious Paragraphs** — Now return to the REPLIES document by selecting the E option on the Opening Menu. You will mark each paragraph as a block and store it as a separate document so you can recall it as often as needed.

The commands you use are on the Block Menu:

Begin block: ^BB or F9

End block: ^BE or Shift-F9

Write block: ^BW plus a filename

Mark each paragraph using the following steps:

1) Place the cursor on the first character of the paragraph and give the begin block command with ^BB or by pressing F9.

2) Move the cursor to the first character of the next paragraph and give the Block End with ^BE or by pressing Shift-F9. The entire paragraph and the blank line following it is marked as a block. You see it highlighted on the screen.

3) To send the marked paragraph to a new document, use the Block Write command with BW. WordStar 2000 asks

```
File to write to?
```

Type the name that corresponds to your handwritten number on the printed copy of the paragraphs and press Return. For the first paragraph, this is T - 1; for the second T - 2; and so on. Repeat these steps to mark and store each of the paragraphs. When you're done, type

```
^QA
```

or pressing Alt-2 to abandon the current document.

**Writing a Letter** — You can now write letters to individuals using the stored paragraphs. Let's assume that you have several letters to answer today. To save time, type all the letters in one file named *TOUR-RES.PON*.

Use the LETTER.FRM format file for the letters. Type today's date and press Return four times to insert blank lines. The first letter goes to

```
Alfonzo Whipple
13448 Alpine Overlook
Green Bay, Wisconsin 53020
Dear Mr. Whipple:
```

Press Return twice. Mr. Whipple has inquired about tours but has not yet submitted a reservation form nor the deposit. Which paragraphs should be included in his letter? Select T-1, T-10 and T-11.

With the cursor positioned two lines below the salutation where paragraph T-1 is to begin, type

```
^BI
```

for Block Insert. WordStar 2000 asks

```
Document to insert?
```

Type

```
T-1
```

or move the highlight bar to T-1, using the Arrow keys. Then press Return. Paragraph T-1 should appear on the screen at the point of the cursor.

Now move the cursor down to the second line below the first paragraph to mark the beginning point of the next paragraph. Repeat the ^BI command to insert paragraph T-10. Finally, move the cursor to the second line below the T-10 paragraph to insert T-11.

**Required Page Break** — The letter to Mr. Whipple is complete. You can now form the next letter by retrieving another set of paragraphs. However, you need to insert a command that tells WordStar 2000 to begin a new page. Type

```
^OP
```

for Option Page. On the screen you see

```
[PAGE]--------------------------------P
```

This is WordStar 2000's notation for the end of a page. The ^OP command requires a new page to begin at this point. It stays in place regardless of how much text is inserted or deleted on the pages preceding or following the command.

**More Letters** — To practice writing letters built from stored paragraphs, write to the following individuals. Select paragraphs appropriate to their status. Don't forget the ^OP command to separate the letters onto four pages.

```
Ms. Alvena Middleton
1330 Sussex Avenue
Needham, Massachusetts 08101
```

Alvena is interested in the archeology tour in Israel, needs special medical considerations, and has not yet paid her deposit.

```
Dr. Emily Dorson
212 North Main Street
Dallas, Texas 75012
```

Emily hasn't decided on a specific tour.

```
Mr. Arvin Ritz
8181 East 18th Circle
Pueblo, Colorado 86613
```

Arvin has submitted his reservation form and deposit for the Computers at Sea Cruise. You are confirming his reservation and reminding him to invite his friends.

**Final Touches**—Before you would print the letters on stationery, remember to allow space at the top for the imprint. Go back now to add blank lines to the top of each letter. Assume that you need two inches at the top of the letter before the date prints. The format already allows one inch in the top margin, so you need to add an additional inch, or six blank lines. Or if each of the letters is only one page long like these are, you can change the format of this document to have a larger top margin by returning to the Opening Menu, using F and then typing

```
TOUR-RES.PON
```

as the formatted document to change.

Save and print the letters you wrote. If you're at the Opening Menu, type

```
P
```

to Print. From within the document, type

```
^QP
```

to Quit and Print or simply use Alt-4, which does the same thing. Compare your printed letters to those in Figure 8-1. How did you do?

**Things to Remember**—What if Dr. Dorson has traveled with Wellington Travel before and you would like to add a personal note to her letter before printing? That's quick and easy. After assembling the paragraphs, simply add a sentence to a paragraph, type an additional paragraph or add a post script to the letter. The stored paragraphs are unaffected by changes you make to them after they are inserted into another document.

The stored paragraph documents are unformatted. They have no margins, page breaks or page numbers, and the text is unjustified. When you marked and wrote them to a new file with the ^BW command, they didn't take with them any of the format commands from the original document. Because the stored paragraphs have no format, they automatically adjust to fit the format of the document into which they are inserted when you use the ^BI command.

May 16, 1985


Alfonzo Whipple
13448 Alpine Overlook
Green Bay, Wisconsin  53020

Dear Mr. Whipple:

WELLINGTON TRAVEL's roster of tours for 1986 is our finest
yet.  Enclosed please find a picture brochure that describes
each of our three major tours.  To assure your reservation,
submit the application form with the deposit required for
the tour of your choice.

Also let me remind you of our special offer.  If you and
three of your friends register for the same tour and pay the
required deposit before October 15, 1985, each of you will
receive a 15% discount on the total tour price!  Never
before has WELLINGTON TRAVEL made such a generous discount
offer.

Sincerely,



Sidney Russet
Tour Coordinator
WELLINGTON TRAVEL

Fig. 8-1/Practice letter #1.

---

May 16, 1985



Ms. Alvena Middleton
1330 Sussex Avenue
Needham, Massachusetts  08101

Dear Ms. Middleton:

Archaeology in Israel, WELLINGTON TRAVEL's most popular
tour, is being repeated in 1986.  This historical adventure
will take you to Israel for three weeks beginning June 4
where you'll see excavation in progress at Beersheba and the
Temple Mount in Jerusalem.  You'll learn about several ancient civilizations as you tour Megiddo, Jericho and Qumran.
Spend a night on a kibbutz in Galilee, wade in the Dead Sea,

Fig. 8-1/Practice letter #2.

take a boat ride on the Sea of Galilee, make a pilgrimage to
the famous Church of the Nativity in Bethlehem and more!

The Archaeology in Israel Tour is filling fast. Although I
already have your reservation form, the reservation is not
confirmed until WELLINGTON TRAVEL receives the deposit.
You'll want to take care of this immediately so you don't
miss this trip of a lifetime.

Due to the physical limitations or special medical needs you
specified on your reservation form, you need to complete the
enclosed medical release form. A portion of the form
requires your doctor's approval for participating in the
tour. Your reservation will be held by the deposit and will
be refunded to you if your physician denies travel approval.

Also let me remind you of our special offer. If you and
three of your friends register for the same tour and pay the
required deposit before October 15, 1985, each of you will
receive a 15% discount on the total tour price! Never
before has WELLINGTON TRAVEL made such a generous discount
offer.

Sincerely,


Sidney Russet
Tour Coordinator
WELLINGTON TRAVEL

Fig. 8-1/Practice letter #2.

May 16, 1985


Dr. Emily Dorson
212 North Main Street
Dallas, Texas  75012

Dear Emily:

WELLINGTON TRAVEL's roster of tours for 1986 is our finest
yet. Enclosed please find a picture brochure that describes

Fig. 8-1/Practice letter #3.

each of our three major tours.  To assure your reservation,
submit the application form with the deposit required for
the tour of your choice.

Also let me remind you of our special offer.  If you and
three of your friends register for the same tour and pay the
required deposit before October 15, 1985, each of you will
receive a 15% discount on the total tour price!  Never
before has WELLINGTON TRAVEL made such a generous discount
offer.

Sincerely,


Sidney Russet
Tour Coordinator
WELLINGTON TRAVEL

Fig. 8-1/Practice letter #3.

May 16, 1985


Mr. Arvin Ritz
8181 East 18th Circle
Pueblo, Colorado  86613

Dear Arvin:

This letter confirms your reservation for the Computers At
Sea cruise in the Hawaiian Islands beginning April 17, 1986.

Also let me remind you of our special offer.  If you and
three of your friends register for the same tour and pay the
required deposit before October 15, 1985, each of you will
receive a 15% discount on the total tour price!  Never
before has WELLINGTON TRAVEL made such a generous discount
offer.

Sincerely,


Sidney Russet
Tour Coordinator
WELLINGTON TRAVEL

Fig. 8-1/Practice letter #4.

Some commands, however, remain with the marked block when you use the
^BW command. These include boldfacing, underlining, centering and similar
commands specifying print characteristics.

## USING WINDOWS TO RECALL STORED TEXT

The previous section showed you how to mark and save individual paragraphs
as separate documents and then recall them. Another way to do this is to use
WordStar 2000's window feature. You will use the paragraphs you typed in the
REPLIES document. However, rather than marking and storing each in a separate
file, you will simply display the REPLIES document in one window on the screen.
You can then mark and copy the desired paragraphs into another window to create
the personalized letters.

**Opening a Window**—Edit the REPLIES document so it is displayed on the
screen. To open another window on the screen for creating the letters, type

^OW

for Option Window or press F3. WordStar 2000 prompts

`Document to edit or create?`

Type

`TOUR-LTR`

using uppercase or lowercase letters. Press Return. Because this is a new
document, you will also need to specify a format. Move the highlight bar to
LETTER.FRM and press Return.

Now you see a second Ruler Line across the middle of the screen. The new
document TOUR-LTR is displayed in the lower half of the screen. The cursor is in
the newly opened window. The document with the paragraphs, REPLIES, is in the
upper window of the screen.

With the cursor in the TOUR-LTR document, type the date, the inside
address and the salutation for the first letter:

```
Alfonzo Whipple
13448 Alpine Overlook
Green Bay, Wisconsin 53020
```

`Dear Mr. Whipple:`

Then move the cursor to the other window that contains the paragraphs. You do
this by typing

^CW

for change window or by pressing Shift-F3. The cursor jumps to the other window.

The first paragraph in the REPLIES document begins the letter to Mr.
Whipple. Mark the first paragraph as a block. With the cursor at the beginning of
the paragraph, type

^BB

or press F9. Then move the cursor to the first character of the next paragraph and mark the end of the block by typing

^BE

or by pressing Shift-F9. The entire paragraph is highlighted to indicate that it is marked. You included the blank line that follows the first paragraph in the block. This blank line will separate the first paragraph from the second one in Mr. Whipple's letter.

**Copying the Block to Another Window**—When the first paragraph is marked, you are ready to copy it to the other window. First, you must move the cursor to the second window by typing

^CW

or by pressing Shift-F3. Move the cursor to the second line below the salutation of the letter. Then give the Block Copy command

^BC

or Shift-F10. A copy of the paragraph in the original document is inserted into Mr. Whipple's letter. Note that the paragraph is copied, not moved, so it is available for repeated use.

Now go back to the upper window to mark another block. Move the cursor to the beginning of paragraph T-10. Mark this paragraph and the closing paragraph, T-11, as a block. You can mark them as one block to save time because they are adjacent.

When the block is marked, change windows and copy the block. As in the previous section, type

^OP

at the end of Mr. Whipple's letter to mark the page break so you can continue with the next letter.

Using windows to recall desired sections of text lets you see the text on the screen before it is inserted into a letter. You might find this more convenient than the first method described. You will appreciate this time-saving feature, whichever procedure you prefer.

## CUSTOMIZING NEARLY IDENTICAL DOCUMENTS

The previous section showed you how to construct unique documents by selecting standard sections of text. In this section you will learn about documents that stay *nearly* the same. Only certain "fill-in-the-blank" information like name, company, address or date varies. The documents you create this way are relatively few in number. Keep in mind that if the volume increases or if the information is already available in a data file—a database file or a MailMerge data file—you will want to use WordStar 2000's MailMerge program.

**Skeleton Document**—To see another way of working with repetitious documents, you will type several paragraphs of a simple will. The majority of the text remains the same, but there are areas requiring you to type a small amount of text. What you type at these points makes each document unique. The skeleton document you create makes your work easier, serving like a fill-in-the-blank form.

To mark the locations of the "blanks," you type an asterisk or another character that is not part of the regular document. For example, if the document includes footnote references using an asterisk, select a character other than the asterisk as the marker.

Once the document is typed, you'll use WordStar 2000's Locate command to find the markers one at a time, giving you the opportunity to fill in the blank. **Designing the Format**—Before typing the will, create a new format named *WILL.FRM.* Design it with double spacing, a 65-character line, tabs set at 10-space increments, and turn off automatic hyphenation, justification, and page numbering. Remember to change the top and bottom margins to three lines and the page length to 33 lines when you select double spacing, 3.00 lines per inch. **Typing the Will**—Create a document named *WILL.STD*—the name identifies it as a standard will—using the WILL.FRM format. Type the text as you see it, using asterisks to mark the fill-in spots. The word immediately following the asterisk helps you identify the kind of text you will later type. Use the center command, ^OC or Shift-F2 to center the heading lines.

```
                  Last Will and Testament
                            of
                          *name
     I, *name , of * County, *state , being of sound mind,
do declare this to be my Last Will and Testament.
     First, as soon as practical after my death, my debts
and expenses of my last illness and funeral shall be paid in
full.
     Then, I hereby give and bequeath all of my personal and
real belongings wherever they may be to *name . Should the
aforementioned individual predecease me, I bequeath all of my
belongings to be equally divided among my surviving children.
     Should I have no surviving children at the time of my
death, my entire estate will be distributed as follows:
     *
     Any beneficiary shall be deemed to have predeceased me
if his or her death occurs within sixty (60) days of mine.
     I appoint *name to serve as the Personal Representative
of this Last Will and Testament. In the event that *name is
unable or unwilling to serve in this capacity, I appoint *name
as Alternate Personal Representative. Further, if both of the
aforementioned individuals are unable or unwilling to serve,
I appoint *name as Second Alternate Personal Representative.
```

```
   In witness whereof, I have hereunto set my hand on this
*date day of *month , *year .

-----------------
*name
Witnesses

----------------- residing at -----------------
                              -----------------
----------------- residing at -----------------
                              -----------------
```

When you've typed the skeleton will document, save it on the disk by typing

`^QS`

or Alt-1.

**Using the Skeleton Document**—Now you are ready to use the standard document to create a will to meet someone's specific need. First, keep in mind that you want to be able to use the stored document repeatedly for generating wills. The document you just typed must remain unchanged, as an "archive" copy always available for preparing another will. To do this, you will put the contents of the WILL.STD document into a new document before making the changes with either the Block Insert or the Copy command.

Both are described below as you prepare a will for Sidney Russet.

**Using Block Insert**—You used this method earlier in the chapter for recalling stored paragraphs. Create a document named *RUSSET.WIL* using the WILL.FRM format. Now type

`^BI`

When WordStar 2000 asks

`Document to insert?`

type

`WILL.STD`

or move the highlight to this document. Then press Return. WordStar 2000 brings the entire standard will into the RUSSET.WIL document. You can now alter the RUSSET.WIL document as you wish without affecting the stored WILL.STD file.

**Using Copy**—Another way to transfer the standard will to another document is to use the Copy command found on the Opening Menu that reappears after you save the WILL.STD document. Type

`C`

for Copy. WordStar 2000 asks

`File to copy from?`

so you type

`WILL.STD`

using either uppercase or lowercase letters. Press Return. Or, you can move the highlight bar to the desired document and press Return. Then WordStar 2000 asks

`File to copy to?`

and you type

`RUSSET.WIL`

and press Return.

The name you type in response to WordStar 2000's second question needs to be a name that you haven't used for a document on the current disk or in the same directory of your hard disk. If you type a name that WordStar 2000 finds on the disk, the program says

`That file already exists - Replace? (Y/N) N`

as a reminder. If you press Y in response to this question, you lose the contents of the earlier file by that name. The contents of the file you copied from replace it.

When the copy is completed, the Opening Menu again appears on the screen. Now type

`E`

to edit the RUSSET.WIL document.

**Personalizing the Will**—To fill in the blanks marked by the asterisks, you will use the Locate command, instructing WordStar 2000 to find the occurrences of the asterisks one at a time. When an asterisk is located, you can remove the asterisk and the word immediately following it before typing the desired text.

**Locate Command**—To give the Locate command, type

`^L`

The command begins at the cursor and continues to the end of the document. Therefore, the cursor needs to be at the beginning of the document to find all of the asterisks. You'll repeat the command to work your way through the document one asterisk at a time.

After you give the Locate command, WordStar 2000 asks a series of questions. The first is

`Text to locate?`

You type

`*`

and press Return. Next you see

`Locate only/Replace? (L/R)`

Type

`L`

and press Return to Locate the asterisk. The R alternative would let you provide replacement text as well. However, you will only locate the text because the information to be inserted at each asterisk is different, making it impossible to tell WordStar 2000 what the replacement text will be.

Next WordStar 2000 asks you to specify the options or conditions under which the text is to be located:

```
Options?
```

Your choices are displayed in a box below the question

```
nth occurrence      Whole words only
Backwards search    Case match
```

**Options**—To use the first choice, `nth occurrence`, type a number as represented by the *n*. For example, if you type 3, WordStar 2000 will locate the third asterisk.

To select one or more of the other options, you simply type the boldfaced letter. Use B to search Backward if the cursor is at the end of the document. Unless you use this option, the search begins at the cursor and continues forward to the end of the document.

Use W to find the text only if it is a whole word. Let's say, for example, that you want to locate the occurrences of *our* in a document. You want WordStar 2000 to find *our* only when it is a whole word but not when *our* is embedded in longer words like *hour, devour* or *poured*.

In this case, use the W option to locate *our* only when is stands as a whole word, with a space before and after it.

Finally, the C option requires WordStar 2000 to locate the word exactly as you type it. If you typed *Our* and use the Case option, WordStar 2000 will locate only the capitalized word. If you typed *our* with the C option in effect, only the lowercase word is found. If the word you are looking for may be either lowercase or uppercase, forego the C option.

So to look for the asterisks in the letter, you won't need any of the options. Just press Return in response to the question.

The first stop the cursor makes is in the heading of the will:

```
                        *name
```

First, remove *name* by typing

```
^RW
```

for Remove Word or press F6. Now type

```
Sidney Russet
```

and notice that this line remains centered. This is because the center command you typed in the skeleton will is still in effect. Now the heading is complete and each line is centered.

To instruct WordStar 2000 to locate the Next asterisk, type

```
^N
```

In the first paragraph, the next asterisk marks the place for you to type the name again. Remove *name* with the Remove Word command (^RW or F6) and type

`Sidney Russet`

and give the Next command again with

`^N`

The next asterisk stands alone, not connected to a word. Delete it and type the name of the county where Sidney resides:

`Cook`

Type

`^N`

again and the cursor stops, asking for the state. Remove *state,* type

`Illinois`

and give the Next command again.

The beneficiary of the estate is named at the next asterisk. Remove the asterisk marker and type

`Albert M. Russet, my father`

in its place.

When WordStar 2000 finds the next asterisk, you will type more detailed information about the division of the estate if the beneficiary is deceased and if Sidney has no surviving children. Remove the asterisk and type

`Fifty percent (50%) to my brother, Walter J. Russet, of Columbus, Ohio, and Fifty percent (50%) to my sister, Lynne M. Brummel, of Evergreen Park, Illinois`

At the next asterisk remove the asterisk and the word immediately following it and type

`Albert M. Russet, my father`

to name him as the Personal Representative. Type

`Joanne Everly, my aunt`

at the next asterisk to be the Alternate Personal Representative. To name the Second Alternate at the next asterisk, type

`Paul J. Russet, my uncle`

Finally, add today's date, month and year to the last paragraph to complete Sidney Russet's will. At this point you can also add more paragraphs to this document that are not usually part of the standard will.

**Using Search and Replace**—To personalize Sidney Russet's will, you used the Locate feature. WordStar 2000 located text, but you had to type the desired replacement text. You can also have WordStar 2000 automatically replace the located text.

Let's say, for example, that the main character in the short story you have written is Benjamin. After reading through the manuscript, you decide that the name *Alex* would better fit the character. Let WordStar 2000 rewrite the story for you!

With the cursor at the beginning of the document, type

```
^L
```

to invoke the Locate command. WordStar 2000 asks a series of questions along the left edge of the screen very similar to the one you saw earlier. To locate *Benjamin* and change it to *Alex,* type responses to the questions until the screen looks like this

```
Text to locate? ............. Benjamin
Locate only/Replace? (L/R) ... R
Replacement Text? ........... Alex
Options?

no. of times to search and replace      Whole words only
Backwards search                        Case match (locate)
Don't ask approval     Show onscreen Preserve case (replace)
```

**Options**—The Locate command that specifies a replacement text displays a different set of options. Again, you can type a number that specifies the number of times the replacement will be made. Like the Locate command without the Replace feature, using W locates text only if it is a whole word. Using B conducts the search backward through the document. Using C requires the located text to match the case of the text you typed.

The last three options are not like those you used when searching for the asterisks in a document. Using D for Don't ask approval gives WordStar 2000 permission to make automatic replacements. If you are fascinated by the moving magic of locate and replace, use S to ask WordStar 2000 to Show each replacement as it is made. When the novelty wears off, omit this option to speed the process. The S option is usable only if you specify the D option.

Normally, when WordStar 2000 makes a replacement, the case of the replacement text matches that of the located text. For example, if *Good* is located, it will be replaced with *Best* and *good* with *best.* Using the final option, P, changes this, letting you Preserve the case of the replacement text just as you typed it. This means that if the replacement word is *best,* and you specify the P option, it will not become *Best* when it replaces *Good.*

In our example, you may not need many of the options. If the cursor is at the end of the story, use B to search backward toward the beginning. You could also choose whether to use D for Don't ask approval and S for Show onscreen.

Now, let's consider another situation. If your character is *Bill* and you want to locate and change his name to *Harold,* you'll want to use the Whole word and Case options. Do this because it is possible to have used *Bill* or *bill* to refer to something other than the character.

For example, one of the characters might mutter, "Bills, bills. I work just to pay the bills." If no options are specified, the sentence will read, "Harolds, harolds. I work just to pay the harolds." That's not quite what you had in mind! If the Whole word option is used alone, the original sentence remains intact. If only the Case option is specified, the sentence becomes "Harolds, bills. I work just to pay the bills."

**Searching for Command Characters**—In response to the Locate question, you can tell WordStar 2000 to find some of the hidden commands that you see in the text when you use ^OD. For example, let's assume that you would like to eliminate all boldface commands from your document and replace them with the underline command.

Turn the Option Display on by typing

^OD

Then you can search for [B] or [b], the codes representing the boldface command. Replace this command with [U] or [u], the underline command. Notice that you can type the B and U in uppercase or lowercase, but WordStar 2000 converts them to uppercase.

**Searching for and Replacing "Wild-Card" Characters**—You can also search for characters that you're unable to specify—so-called "wild-card" characters. For example, you want to locate all references to any date in the 1970s—you don't care which year it is specifically. In response to the Locate question, type

197[#]

with the [#] representing any number. Be sure to include the brackets. Otherwise, WordStar 2000 will literally look for 197#, something you likely didn't put in your document.

To search for another unspecified character, use [?]. For example, if you search for

s[?]w

WordStar 2000 will locate words like *saw, sew,* and *sow*—words that begin with *s,* end with *w* and have just one character between. If you search for

s[?][?]w

WordStar 2000 locates words like *snow* and *slew.*

## SUMMARY

In this chapter you have learned to use the Block Insert, Copy, Locate, and Locate/Replace commands to make your work easier. These commands can be used specifically for creating repetitious documents, but you can also use them whenever they'll save typing time.

# Typing Outlines & Indented Text  9

The unique characteristics of an outline format are the indentation and alignment of text. Generally, the letters and numbers marking each point of an outline heading extend to the left of each line of the explanatory text. If the explanatory text is more than one line long, each line wraps to align below the previous line rather than returning to the left margin.

The principles of an outline format are shared with other kinds of documents too. Many times you want to include numbered or lettered paragraphs in a memo or letter. Like the outline, the numbers or letters print at the left margin or some other specified point. The paragraphs that follow are indented. The format that extends the first line of a paragraph or section, while indenting subsequent lines is sometimes called a *hanging indent*.

Another time you use indented text is in an article or research paper. An extended quote may be indented—and sometimes single-spaced—to set it apart from the surrounding text. In this case there is no preceding letter or number. The indent used for this kind of text is sometimes referred to as a *temporary left margin*. Until the command is cancelled, WordStar 2000 recognizes the indent as the beginning point for each line—the place lines begin when lines are wrapped.

Another option WordStar 2000 offers is the ability to indent sections of quotations from both the left and right, setting temporary left and right margins.

Whatever your writing task—your breakfast club speech outline, a research paper for your history class, a magazine article, or a book—you'll likely find frequent uses for the indent format.

## INDENTED TEXT MADE EASY

WordStar 2000 has several features that make the indent format easy to work with. First, the indentations are displayed on the screen as they will print. This removes any guesswork from the formatting process. You rearrange the text until it appears on the screen just as you want it on paper.

The indents in effect are highlighted on the Ruler Line at the top of the window. This lets you know exactly how the text you're about to type will be indented.

Unlike the older WordStar, WordStar 2000 stores tab and margin settings with the document so there's no need to reset these commands during a subsequent editing session. The next time you work on the document with outline and indent commands in it, WordStar 2000 remembers how the text is formatted. The tab and indent commands are hidden in the document, keeping the document in the proper format while you add or delete text. Each time the cursor crosses an embedded Ruler Line or an indent command, the Ruler Line at the top of the screen or window changes to match the hidden commands.

WordStar 2000's window feature used in the previous chapter is another benefit when working with outlines. As you write a paper, report, article, or book chapter, you can refer to a copy of your outline displayed in a second window. If as you write you discover that the outline needs rearranging, you can move the cursor to the window with the outline to make the necessary changes. Then return to the text document to resume writing.

As you can see, getting the most out of the indent feature uses three important ingredients—tabs, indents and windows. Tabs and indents are the subject of this chapter. Let's look at how they complement each other when you prepare documents.

## THE IMPORTANCE OF TABS

Tab settings—the small triangles on the Ruler Line—mark the points of indentation. The tabs you set determine the size of the indentation or the location of the temporary left margin. If you plan to indent a line five spaces, you must have a tab set five spaces from the left margin. If lines are to indent five spaces from both the left and right margins, you must have a tab five spaces from each margin.

**Outline Format**—You can set tabs while designing the format file. These tabs are set at evenly-spaced intervals. You have already created several format files, so recall that you type

F

at the Opening Menu. Name this format *OUTLINE.FRM* and respond to the questions.

Specify 6.00 lines per inch for single spacing, set the right margin at 60, and accept the default that sets tabs every five spaces. You can exercise your preference on justification, automatic hyphenation, underlining and page numbering.

If you need to go through the questions again to make more changes, type

`C`

Then when the format is the way you want it, save it by typing

`S`

**Indent Document**—When the Opening Menu appears on the screen, press

`E`

to Edit a document. Type

`INDENT.DOC`

in either uppercase or lowercase letters and press Return. You are creating a new document named *INDENT.DOC* that you will use for practicing the indent command in this chapter. When WordStar 2000 asks:

`Format to use?`

move the highlight bar to *OUTLINE.FRM* and press Return.

**Changing Tabs in a Document**—When you are working in the document, tabs can be further changed as necessary using the Tabs and Margins Menu. Type

`^TS`

to set a tab or press F8. WordStar 2000 then asks

`Set tab in what column?`

and provides the column number of cursor's position at the time you gave the command. Type the desired number and press Return. Repeat this command until the desired tabs are set.

**Clearing Tabs in a Document**—Of course, you may also need to remove unwanted tab settings. Again, the command is in the Tabs and Margins Menu

`^TC`

for Tab Clear or press Shift-F8. Then type the column number of the tab to be eliminated when WordStar 2000 prompts

`Clear tab in what column? (A for ALL)`

Again, the number WordStar 2000 supplies is the cursor's position at the time you gave the command. Typing

`A`

and pressing Return removes all tabs. Of course, if you want to remove all tabs and start over, you'd want to give this command *before* taking the time to set up any tabs as described earlier!

## INDENT COMMANDS

Before typing a document using the indent commands, let's preview the commands you'll use to have WordStar 2000 format the document as you want it. These commands are on the Tabs and Margins Menu so they all begin with ^T.

**Tab Indent**—Use ^TI or F5. This sets a temporary left margin at the next tab setting. WordStar 2000 inserts the code [TI] to mark each indent command.

**Tab Outdent**—Use ^TO or Shift-F5. This sets the temporary left margin at the previous tab setting. WordStar 2000 inserts the code [TO] to mark the place the command was given.

**Tab Both**—Use ^TB to set a temporary margin to the next tab on both left and right sides. WordStar 2000 inserts the code [TB].

**Tab Undo**—Use ^TU to undo or cancel all indent commands. WordStar 2000 inserts the code [TU].

**In General**—You will use the Tab Indent (^TI or F5) command once to indent text to the first tab setting. Repeating the command increases the indent to the next tab setting.

The indent stays in place when you press Return. This makes it possible for you to type several paragraphs using the same indentation format. The indent takes effect at the cursor line when the command is given and continues until another command changing the size of the indent or cancelling it is given.

**If You're Familiar With WordStar**—WordStar 2000's indent command is similar to the original WordStar's ^OG command. Repeating the command in the older version increased the size of the indentation to the next tab stop, a feature retained in WordStar 2000.

However, there are two primary differences. First, the indent command in WordStar 2000 is not cancelled by pressing Return as was the case in WordStar. To cancel the indent, you must deliberately give a command.

Second, the indent command is embedded in the text so it will remain in effect even when margins change. For example, let's say that you typed a document using the default left margin of 1 and the default tab setting with the first tab in column 6. You give the indent command once so a paragraph will be indented five spaces from the left margin to the first tab setting. Then let's assume you later change the left margin. The indent command will still indent text to the first tab setting from the left margin. Note that the indent may no longer be exactly five spaces from the left margin as it originally was. This is because the first tab may not be exactly five spaces from the new left margin. The text will, however, be indented to the first tab to the right of the left margin.

## USING INDENTS

Let's look at brief examples that illustrate different ways to use the indent commands:

**Hanging Indent**—Remember that the characteristic of the hanging indent is the first line of a paragraph extending to the left of the other lines in the paragraph. Entries in a bibliography are examples of the hanging indent:

```
Adrian, Vivienne. The Wonderful World of Word Processing.
     Helena, MT: Excellent Press, 1984. 164 pp.
```

```
Type, Tella. Developing a Way With Words. Springfield, IL:
     Tella Publishing, 1984. 64 pp.
```

```
Zorta, Tim. The Art of Biography Writing. Nowata, OK: Delmar
     and Sons, Inc., 1983. 256 pp.
```

To do this, type the author's name

```
Adrian, Vivienne.
```

in the first entry. Now give the indent command by typing

```
^TI
```

or pressing F5. Continue typing the bibliographic entry. Notice that when the text is wrapped to the second line, the cursor moves to the first tab setting marked by the highlight on the Ruler Line.

When you have finished typing the first entry, you must cancel the indent command. Do this by typing

```
^TO
```

for Tab Outdent or by pressing Shift-F5. This lets you begin the second entry at the left margin.

Now type the remaining two entries, giving the indent command once when the cursor has passed the first tab position and remembering to cancel the command at the end of each entry.

The examples in this chapter are brief so type them into the same file as though they are one document. To separate this example from the next one you will create, give the page break command by typing

```
^OP
```

for Option Page break.

**Numbered Paragraphs** — Another common use of the indent commands creates numbered paragraphs within a document. For example, the tour plans offered by Wellington Travel could be summarized in a numbered format for use in a letter, memo or brochure.

```
1. Computers at Sea. A one-week cruise in the Hawaiian
   Islands with several hours of hands-on computer
   training each day.

   Nationally prominent computer trainers and lecturers
   lead the seminars covering word processing, electronic
   spreadsheet, database and business graphics topics.

2. Archaeology in Israel. This three-week tour includes
   visits of several prominent archaeological sites
   including Jerusalem and Megiddo. Sightseeing in
   Jericho, Jerusalem, Haifa and a night on a kibbutz in
   Galilee are included.
```

```
3.  Music and Art Tour of Europe. This 18-day tour of
    Europe includes castles, cathedrals, and art museums in
    England, France, Germany, Switzerland, Austria and
    Italy. This tour appropriately celebrates the 301st
    birthdays of musicians Johann Sebastian Bach and George
    Frederick Handel in 1986.
```

Typing numbered paragraphs is very similar to creating the hanging indents in the bibliographical entries. The primary difference is that you will press the Tab key to insert the space between the number and the text. Here's how you do it:

First, type the number and the period following it:

```
1.
```

Press the Tab key to move the cursor to the first tab. Now give the indent command by typing

```
^TI
```

or by pressing F5. Type the paragraph and you see each line of the paragraph wrap starting at the tab setting. If you elected to use automatic hyphenation feature, the line breaks may be different on your screen than you see them printed in this book.

Because pressing Return does not cancel the indent command, you can continue typing the unnumbered indented paragraph that follows the first paragraph without repeating the command.

However, at the end of the unnumbered paragraph you need to cancel the indent command by typing

```
^TO
```

or by pressing Shift-F5. Type the number to begin the next paragraph and press the Tab key to move the cursor to the first tab setting. Type the paragraph as you did earlier and give the Outdent command at the end. Repeat these steps for the remaining paragraph also.

Again, type

```
^OP
```

to insert a page break to begin the next example.

**Left and Right Indents**—As mentioned earlier in the chapter, you might indent text on both the left and right margins if you were including an extended quotation in a document. You might also use this indent option to create a question-and-answer format:

```
Must I pay WELLINGTON TRAVEL the entire tour price in
advance of departure?
                    A deposit is required to hold your
                    reservation when application is made.
                    The balance of the payment is due no
                    later than 21 days before departure.
                    Remember, we accept most charge cards.
```

Are there special rates for groups traveling together?

>For the first time this year, WELLINGTON
>TRAVEL is offering a special discount.
>If you and three of your friends pay the
>required deposit before October 15, each
>of you will receive an additional 15%
>discount from our already competitive
>prices.

To do this, type the question without using an indent command. Press Return twice to move the cursor to the line where the answer starts. Now give the command that indents text on both the left and right margins,

^TB

twice so the answer section is indented two tab stops from each margin.

After typing the answer section, undo all the indent commands by typing

^TU

and you're ready to type the next question.

Notice that you need to use the Tab Undo command, ^TU, to cancel the command that indents on both the left and right margins. The ^TO or Shift-F5 command you used earlier affects only the left side of the text.

If you were to type the ^TO command twice in this example rather than using ^TU, the left margin would return to its original setting. But the temporary right margin would be retained. The ^TU command could be used in lieu of the ^TO commands in the previous examples to quickly undo all previously set indents.

**Combining Indent Commands**—You can combine the left and right indent commands. This is useful for formatting a script, for example:

Narrator: The birthday party for a city is a reason for
celebration. It has been blanketed by the winter
snows and scorched by the summer sun for 150
years. Now we gather to celebrate the marvel of
its survival and prosperity.

>A lone bearded man dressed in a
>dark coat and boots enters the
>dark stage. A spot light
>follows him as he sits on a
>rock under a tree in center
>stage. He is silent and
>contemplative.

Narrator: Some things haven't changed. The mountains still
guard our skyline as they did when the first
settlers arrived the early 1800s. The rivers,
although not as unblemished as our forefathers saw
them, still flow through our city. As monuments
to progress and civilization, man has dotted the

```
                 landscape with skyscrapers and smoke stacks of
                 industry.
                     Slowly the lights increase.
                     People dressed representing the
                     eras of the city-past and
                     modern-enter and surround the
                     lone figure on the stage.
```

To do this, indent the narrator's section two tabs on the left. The interspersed explanatory paragraphs are indented three tab settings on both the left and right. You have used these commands separately in the previous examples. This time you will mix them in the same exercise. Type

```
Narrator:
```

and press Tab. Now give the Indent command twice so all the lines of the paragraph will align at this tab. Type

```
^TI
```

twice or simply press F5 twice and type the first paragraph. After typing the narrator's paragraph, type

```
^TU
```

to Undo all indent commands.

You want the second paragraph to be indented on both sides so you type

```
^TB
```

three times to indent three tab spaces from each margin. Notice how the highlight marks this command on both ends of the Ruler Line. Type the second paragraph. When it is finished, give the

```
^TU
```

command to again cancel all the indent commands. Continue typing the next narrator's section and the final explanatory paragraph just as you did the first two.

To mark the end of this exercise, type

```
^OP
```

to start a new page.

**Outlines**—Of course, indent commands are useful for creating outlines. To indent the subpoints, you simply give an additional indent command. As with creating numbered paragraphs, this feature is helpful when the explanatory text following each point of the outline is more than one line long:

```
            WELLINGTON TRAVEL PROMOTION PLANS

   I.    Advertising

         A.    Daily Reporter:    special rates for Thursday and
               Sunday editions
         B.    Bulk rate flyers to residences
```

```
II. Speaker Service
        A.   Breakfast Clubs:   encourage employee membership in
             breakfast clubs
        B.   Community Service Organizations:   contact program
             coordinators
        C.   Travel Film Socials
             1.   Free public library film series
             2.   Senior citizen centers:   Centre, Newtown,
                  Kirbyville, McPheerson
III. Corporate Client Contacts
        A.   Phone calls to travel directors of regular
             accounts
        B.   "This is Wellington Travel" brochure to
             infrequent customers and prospects
        C.   Personal visits as requested
```

To do this, type the heading

```
WELLINGTON TRAVEL PROMOTION PLANS
```

and center it by typing

```
^OC
```

or by pressing Shift-F2. Then type

```
I.
```

press the Tab key and type

```
Advertising
```

followed by a Return. Now type

```
^TI
```

for Tab Indent or simply press F5 once. When you type

```
A.
```

the letter aligns at the first tab. Now press the Tab key to move the cursor to the next tab setting. Give the Tab Indent command again so the explanatory text will start at this tab. Notice that the highlight on the Ruler Line moves to the second tab setting.

Type

```
Daily Reporter:   special rates for Thursday and Sunday
editions
```

and press Return. When text wraps to the second line, it automatically aligns directly below the first line.

Now you need to "outdent" the left margin one tab stop to type the next item

```
B.
```

Type

`^TO`

for Tab Outdent or press Shift-F5. The highlight on the Ruler Line moves to the previous tab setting. Now type

`B.`

Then press the Tab key to move the cursor to the next tab setting. Because this text is only one line long, you don't need to give another indent command. Type

`Bulk rate flyers to residences`

Then press Return twice. To place the cursor at the left margin, outdent the left margin again by typing

`^TO`

or Shift-F5. An alternative to this command is

`^TU`

to undo all indents.

Now you're ready to type the next point of the outline.

Notice that point C has further subpoints. After typing the level indicator—a Roman numeral, letter or number—remember to press the Tab key to move the cursor to the next Tab setting. Repeat the indent command until the highlight on the Ruler Line marks the desired tab setting. Then to move back toward the left margin to a previous tab, use `^TO` or Shift-F5 command. To return to the left margin to continue with another Roman numeral point, Undo the indents with `^TU`.

If you give the indent command at the beginning of the line before typing any text, you don't need to press the Tab key to move the cursor. When you begin typing, the text automatically jumps to the indent location.

This chapter provided you with an overview of the things that can be done with the indent commands. They are used to set temporary margins on the left or both the left and right. Using the indent commands makes WordStar 2000 responsible for maintaining the alignment of indented text. It does this more accurately and more easily than you could do by manually using the Tab key and repeatedly resetting the margins.

The next chapter is a logical continuation of this one. For example, after you have developed an outline for a research paper or speech, you would write it by adding "flesh" or text to the outline. We will look at inserting footnotes and endnotes into the document. You will also be introduced to the sort feature, which puts the bibliography or other lists in order within your document.

# Writing 10
# A Research Paper

In the last chapter you learned about creating an outline, the important planning step before writing any well-organized document. Many times, writing the outline is the most difficult step. And once your organization and thoughts are on paper, the writing becomes easier.

In this chapter, we'll assume that your writing project is a research paper. If this is a thesis or dissertation for completing a university degree program, you will probably need to write to a rigidly prescribed format. Typically, guidelines are set for top, bottom and side margins. References, footnotes, and the bibliography must be typed in a certain way.

I have heard students who have completed the requirements of an advanced degree program recount their experiences with a "ruler-wielding inspector." This person's sole job seems to be to measure and scrutinize the spacing and format on each page of the completed paper. Although a committee of faculty examiners may have approved the content and the research, the degree could not granted until the paper met the format requirements of the institution.

Granted, not all writing projects are so carefully examined. A research paper for a high-school literature class or an analysis of the writings of an early Greek philosopher may be prepared in approximately the same format. However, the acceptability of these papers does not usually depend on total consistency of all formatting details.

Even so, when precision is necessary, you need to know how to make WordStar 2000 perform at its finest. That is the intent of this chapter.

## SPECIAL NEEDS OF A RESEARCH PAPER

A research paper characteristically includes numerous details that are not a part of less scholarly or less detailed documents. Frequently, a research paper requires footnotes or endnotes. A *footnote* prints at the bottom of a page to cite a reference made in the text. For example, if you state that your research directly contradicts that of Tim Zorta, you will name the published source of Zorta's research. To check the facts and make a comparison between your work and Zorta's, the reader refers to the footnote to obtain information about your source—the publication name and date.

*Endnotes* perform the same functions as footnotes. However, rather than printing at the bottom of the page where they are referenced, endnotes print as a group at the end of the section, chapter, or paper. WordStar 2000 does endnoting—but calls it *footnoting*—for you automatically. Entries are automatically renumbered as necessary when you add and delete references.

Generally, a research paper also has an extensive bibliography that lists all of your sources. The previous chapter illustrated the use of the hanging indent for formatting bibliographic entries. You can also use WordStar 2000's sort feature to quickly alphabetize or numerically order these lists.

Finally, the research paper requires exact top, bottom and side margins. Guidelines carefully specify the placement of the page number. These are the some of the challenges that await WordStar 2000 when you prepare a research paper. Let's continue to see how it's done.

## FORMATTING

Designing the correct format is a two-step process. First, you will peruse the published style guide to locate formatting specifications. Colleges and universities publish such booklets specifying thesis and dissertation formats. If a document is to be submitted camera-ready for publication, the publisher provides guidelines for printing too.

You might encounter descriptions like this:

1) The title page and chapter titles begin 2-1/2 inches from the top of the page.

2) The page number for the first page of each chapter or section prints centered at the bottom at least one inch from the bottom of the page.

3) Subsequent pages are numbered at the right margin a double space above the first line of text, which starts 1-1/2 inches from the top of the page.

4) The left and top margins must be 1-1/2 inches, the right and bottom margins must be at least one inch.

5) Paragraph indentations are eight spaces.

After extracting the relevant measurements, you're ready for the second step—translating these inches and lines into formatting commands WordStar 2000 understands. Some of these can be controlled by the stored format you create. Others will be set once you begin typing the research paper.

**Stored Format**—You will design the format as generically as possible allowing you to fine-tune the settings once you begin typing. A generic format will impose the fewest number of restrictions when you change from title page to the first page of a chapter to succeeding pages. Each has its own design, yet they have some factors, such as margins, in common.

You will create a stored format called *RESEARCH.FRM.* Let's review the questions you must answer to create this format. Because you're already familiar with these questions, they are abbreviated here rather than being directly quoted from what you will see on the screen.

Font: You will probably use either 10 or 12 characters per inch. Because your paper likely requires letter-quality printing, your printer may offer you the option of proportional spacing, which will be included in your choices on the screen.

Lines per inch: 3.00 for double spacing.

Lines in top margin: 3 to set a top margin of one inch when text is double-spaced.

Lines in bottom margin: 3 to set a bottom margin of one inch when text is double-spaced.

Right margin: 60, which assumes 10 characters per inch and paper 8-1/2 inches wide. The left margin is 1-1/2 inches (15 characters) and the right margin is 1 inch (10 characters). The total page width is 85 characters. Therefore, the space left for text is 85 less the space for margins (15 and 10), leaving 60 characters. If you are using 12 pitch, the same settings apply. The Ruler Line actually measures the page in inches rather than characters. You make the settings as though you were using 10 pitch. WordStar 2000 recalculates the changes if you request 12 pitch.

Tab set every n spaces: Because the style calls for eight-character paragraph indents, you'll set the tabs every eight spaces rather than using the 5 default.

Lines per page: Because you selected double spacing (3.00 lines per inch), lines per page becomes 33.

Even page offset: 15 for 1-1/2 inch left margin. This allows you to leave the left margin at 1 in the document.

Odd page offset: 15 for 1-1/2 inch left margin.

Justified or Ragged J/R: The choice is yours. If your paper includes columns or tables, you may want to use the Ragged option. Justification can also be turned off or on once inside a document by typing ^OJ.

Automatic hyphenation Y/N: Again, the choice is yours. Permitting automatic hyphenation usually gives you a nicer looking document. When you're typing, you can control hyphenation by inserting conditional hyphens at syllable breaks or typing the command in front of the word to prevent hyphenation. As noted before, WordStar 2000 doesn't have a command to turn hyphenation off and on inside the document.

Use form feeds Y/N: This depends on your printer.

Underline between words Y/N: Your preference, but usually the Y default is acceptable.

Display page breaks Y/N: Accept the Y default.

Page-number position: Select N for None. You will control page numbering with header and footer commands.

This completes your generic format. Now let's prepare samples of the different kinds of pages and formats you need for the research paper. We will consider each of the parts of the paper in the order they will appear in the finished product, even though you likely will not actually type them in this order. For example, you can't complete the Table of Contents until the paper is printed and page numbering is complete.

To follow the examples, create a document named *WPTHESIS* using the RESEARCH.FRM format you just set up.

### TYPING THE TITLE PAGE

The Title Page is the first page of the paper displaying the title of the paper, your name, the course name or department and college, and the date. The finished page will look like Figure 10-1.

**Doing It**—First, because some of the lines are single-spaced and some of the specifications are defined in single-spaced lines, you need to change the line spacing for this page from the double-spacing format in effect.

With the cursor at the top of the page, type

```
^PH
```

for Print Height. When the choices are displayed, move the highlight bar to 6.00 for single spacing and press Return. WordStar 2000 inserts the line-spacing command that overrides the information in the stored format. The entire document will now be single-spaced until another command is given to return to double-spacing.

Now you're ready to determine on which line of the page the title will print when the instructions say 2-1/2 inches from the top of the page. You know that the top margin set in the format is 3 double-spaced lines—also equal to 6 single-spaced lines—or one inch. So you need to move down another 1-1/2 inches to leave the 2-1/2 top margin. Some quick calculation tells you that the cursor needs to be on line 10—1.5 inches times 6 lines per inch equals 9 lines for the top margin.

You will center each line after typing it with the ^OC command or by using Shift-F2. Type the first line of the title in all caps:

```
A STUDY OF THE PERCEIVED EFFECTS OF WORD PROCESSING
```

Press Return twice to double-space the title and type the second line.

```
ON JOB SATISFACTION AND FULFILLMENT
```

Press Return three times and type

```
by
```

Press Return twice and type

```
Sidney Rene Russet
```

A STUDY OF THE PERCEIVED EFFECTS OF WORD PROCESSING

ON JOB SATISFACTION AND FULFILLMENT

by

Sidney Rene Russet

---

A Thesis Submitted to the Faculty of the

DEPARTMENT OF BUSINESS ADMINISTRATION

In Partial Fulfillment of the Requirements
For the Degree of

MASTER OF ARTS
WITH A MAJOR IN TRAVEL MANAGEMENT

In the Graduate College

THE UNIVERSITY OF BARLOW

1 9 8 5

Fig. 10-1/Sample title page.

or your name. Press Return seven times to move the cursor to approximately the center of the page top to bottom. Press the underline key 20 times. Center this line also.

Press Return eight times to move the cursor down again and type

`A Thesis Submitted to the Faculty of the`

press Return twice and type

`DEPARTMENT OF BUSINESS ADMINISTRATION`

and press Return twice. Then type

`In Partial Fulfillment of the Requirements`

press Return once and continue with

`For the Degree of`

and press Return twice.

The next two lines are single-spaced

`MASTER OF ARTS`
`WITH A MAJOR IN TRAVEL MANAGEMENT`

Press Return twice and continue with

`In the Graduate College`

press Return twice and type

`THE UNIVERSITY OF BARLOW`

Press Return four times and type the date with a space between each digit:

`1 9 8 5`

Type

`^OP`

to mark this as a required end of page.

**How Did You Do?** — Move the cursor back through this page to verify that you centered each line of text. To check your accuracy, print the page and measure to be sure the desired spacing was achieved. If it didn't come out exactly right, make the necessary revisions in the document. Also check to see that the paper was properly aligned in the printer.

The centered text on the printed page may look uncentered. Remember that the page offset is 15 spaces, or 1-1/2 inches. When you give the center command, text is centered between the margins, not the edges of the paper.

## TYPING THE FRONT MATTER

The *front matter* includes preliminary material necessary to make the paper useful. But these items are not really a part of the report. This includes things like an abstract, acknowledgments, a dedication, and a statement or copyright page. The format for each of these will usually follow that of the first page of a chapter, discussed a little later. Some of the pages are single spaced and others are double-spaced, really a minor—and easily adjusted—difference.

However, a peculiarity of the front matter is that it is numbered sequentially in lowercase Roman numerals. Because WordStar 2000 cannot count in Roman numerals, you will need to use the header and footer commands for properly placing the page numbers.

As an example of the front matter, let's look at typing the Table of Contents. This is an appropriate place to mention the StarIndex program included in the WordStar 2000 Plus package. StarIndex allows you to mark headings and subheadings to be included in the Table of Contents—or an Index as the name implies—and the list or index is created for you. Because Part II of this book discusses only the features of WordStar 2000, it extends beyond the scope of this chapter. The advanced features of WordStar 2000 Plus form the essence of Part III.

**Table of Contents and Other Lists**—A Table of Contents or other lists—such as a List of Illustrations or List of Figures—is quite easy to type. Of course, if you used StarIndex to perform this task for you, it would not be necessary for you to manually hunt through the printed pages to locate chapter titles, subheadings, figure or illustration titles and page numbers. In any case, once the hunting is done, the list is ready to type.

**Roman Numeral Page Numbering**—Let's say that the Table of Contents page will be numbered as lowercase Roman numeral iii. To do this, put the cursor at the top of the page and define a footer by typing

^OF

for Option Footer. When WordStar 2000 prompts for the footer placement, type

B

to print it on both odd and even pages. In reality, you will use this footer only on this one page. If the Table of Contents is more than one page long, the next page is numbered Roman numeral iv, but it will be a header, not a footer. The footer would need to be cancelled on the next page.

When you see the footer brackets on the screen

[FOOTER]

[FOOTER]

you're ready to type the text of the footer, which is simply Roman numeral iii centered on the page. Column 30 would be the centered space between the 60-column margin setting. Because you have three characters in the footer, move the cursor to column 29 and type

iii

Move the cursor outside the brackets and the footer is defined.

You recall that WordStar 2000 automatically leaves a blank line between the text and the first line of the footer. This exactly matches the specifications required for this research-paper format. If, for example, the format had specified two blank lines between the text and the page number, you would have pressed

Return once after the cursor was between the footer command brackets before typing the Roman numeral page number.

**Second Table of Contents Page**—Now let's assume that the Table of Contents continues to page iv. This requires you to do two things. First, the page number shifts to a header printing in the upper right of the page. Second, the footer must be cancelled or `iii` will print at the bottom of the page iv as well.

To work properly, the header command must be given at the top of the page where it is to begin. So, you would position the cursor at the beginning of line 1 on the second Table of Contents page. Give the header command

`^OH`

for Option Header. Again, tell WordStar 2000 that you want this header on both odd and even pages, even though you'll actually use it only on this page.

When the header brackets appear

`[HEADER]`

`[HEADER]`

you'll leave the cursor on the blank line and press the Spacebar to move the cursor to column 59. Type

`iv`

and then move the cursor outside the command brackets. The page number iv will print in columns 59 and 60, placing the last character even with the right margin on the page. Again, WordStar 2000 automatically inserts one blank line between the header and the first line of text, exactly matching the prescribed format.

If the format had called for two blank lines, for example, you would have typed the `iv` for the page number, then pressed Return once to include another blank line in the header.

Next, you need to cancel the footer command that was set on the first page of the Table of Contents. Immediately following the header command, give the footer command again by typing

`^OF`

At the prompt, type

`B`

so the command will apply to both odd and even pages. When the footer command brackets appear, leave them blank. You are creating a blank footer to replace and cancel the footer that previously existed.

After setting the header and footer for the page, you would type the second page of the table of contents. When it is done, type

`^OP`

again to begin a new page.

## THE FIRST CHAPTER

The first page of each chapter has some things in common with the Title and Table of Contents pages. Again, the first line of the page—the chapter number—prints 2-1/2 inches from the top of the page. Like the Table of Contents page, the page number for the first page of each chapter prints centered at the bottom.

The page number for the remaining pages of the chapter prints at the right margin, separated by a blank line from the first line of text.

**First Page of the Chapter**—At the top of the first page, cancel the header command that is still in effect from the previous section. Type

^OH

and leave the text area blank.

As calculated for the Title Page, you'll start typing on line 10. Type the title of the first chapter as follows, centering each line after typing it

CHAPTER 1

press Return twice. Type

THE PROBLEM

Press Return three times to move the cursor where the text will begin. Because the text of the paper will be double spaced, you need to give the appropriate command before you begin typing. You recall that the format you designed specified double spacing. However, at the top of the Title Page you changed to single spacing to permit some of the lines there to be single spaced. The single-spacing command remained in effect for the Table of Contents in the front matter as well.

Now, however, the body of the thesis will be double-spaced. Do you remember the command to change line spacing? Type

^PH

then move the highlight to 3.00 when the list of choices displays, and press Return. WordStar 2000 stores the command in the document so the text following will be double-spaced.

The format also specified that each paragraph would be indented eight spaces. When you designed the RESEARCH.FRM format, you used 8 as the interval for tab settings. The Ruler Line on the screen now reflects that format.

**Page Number**—Again, you need to cancel the header in effect by giving the header command and leaving the space between the markers blank. The footer for this page needs to print the page number centered at the bottom of the first page of the chapter. To do this, give the footer command

^OF

when the cursor is at the beginning of the first line of the first page of a chapter.

When the footer command brackets appear, move the cursor to middle of the line, column 30, by pressing the Spacebar. Then type

&%PAGE&

the code WordStar 2000 understands for printing the page number. The first digit of the page number will print at the location of the first character of the page-number code.

However, what will happen during printing this example if you type &%PAGE& beginning in column 30 to mark the position for the page number? During printing, the first page of chapter 1 would be numbered 3—not exactly what you anticipated when your guidelines state that the first chapter begins consecutive numbering with Arabic numerals. You want 1, not 3.

Why would you get 3? WordStar 2000 kept a record of the number of pages you had typed. It considered the Title Page as 1, the Table of Contents as 2, and now you finally gave it permission to print the page number. Because this is the third page of the document, WordStar 2000 deduced that it should be printed as page 3. Notice that even the Status Line of your screen says you are on page 3.

If you want to use the &%PAGE& command to specify the page number in the footer, you also need the ^OA to clear up the page numbering "misunderstanding" with WordStar 2000. Put the cursor at the top of the page following the header and footer commands and type

^OA

for Option Assign page number. WordStar 2000 asks

Page number to assign?

You type

1

so WordStar 2000 understands that you now want numbering to begin with 1, regardless of the number of pages that actually precede this point in the document.

Keep in mind that the page number on the Status Line of the screen or window remains unchanged even if you use the ^OA command to change the page numbering sequence. Even though the first page of chapter 1 will be numbered 1 during printing, the Status Line still reports that this is page 3 of the document. **Another Option**—After giving the footer command, you could have typed 1 in column 30 as the text for the footer. This would be an acceptable option to print the page number at the bottom of the page. However, this does not set a beginning point for the numbering sequence. In other words, this does not tell WordStar 2000 that the next page should be numbered 2, the next 3, and so on.

The ensuing instructions assume that you used the ^OA command to set the page numbering sequence.

## SUCCESSIVE CHAPTER PAGES

Like the second page of a Table of Contents, the second and all other pages in a chapter need to be numbered at the upper right. So at the top of the second page you need to do two things—give a header command and cancel the footer command that you gave on the first page.

**Header Command for Numbering Pages**—With the cursor at the top of page 2, type

`^OH`

for Option Header. Because you need to be able to move the cursor to column 60 to type the page-numbering code, you need to place a Ruler Line in the header.

Without setting a new right margin, the &%PAGE& code wraps to the next line of the header. Set the right margin at 70. Type

`^TR`

or press Shift-F7, followed by 70 and Return when prompted for a number. This Ruler Line affects only the header. The right margin in the document remains the same.

Now move the cursor to column 60 and type

`&%PAGE&`

This tells WordStar 2000 to replace the code with the actual page number during printing. Because you set the page numbering on the previous page to begin with 1, WordStar 2000 now knows that this page will be 2. During printing the &%PAGE& code is replaced with 2. On the next page, this code in the header is printed as 3 and so on.

**Cancelling the Footer Command**—Like the second page of the Table of Contents, the second page of the chapter must have the command to cancel the footer set on the previous page. With the cursor at the top of the page, give the footer command

`^OF`

Now simply leave the space between the footer commands blank.

## TYPING ENDNOTES

The feature described here as endnotes are called *footnotes* in the WordStar 2000 manuals. You remember that endnotes print collectively at the end of the document. This is the function performed by WordStar 2000's so-called footnote feature. Actual footnotes, on the other hand, print at the bottom of the page on which they are referenced. This feature can be accomplished with WordStar 2000, but must be done manually as you type.

**Creating an Endnote**—Let's say that you are typing your research paper and you made the following statement:

```
Although little research has been done to study the
relationship between the use of word processors and job
satisfaction, literature seems to support the early findings
of Massone and Jensen.
```

Leave the cursor in the space just past the period ending the sentence. At this point you want to cite the publication reporting the research of Massone and Jensen. Rather than including this reference in the document, the information is provided in the endnote. Should the reader wish to check the specifics of this research, the endnote provides the publication name, date and page number.

To type the reference for an endnote type

`^ON`

for Option Note. WordStar 2000 displays a pair of command markers like this:

`[FOOTNOTE 1]`

`[FOOTNOTE 1]`

somewhat like the header and footer command markers. The first marker marks the cursor position at the time the command is given. The last marker is at the left margin, so they may not be vertically aligned on the screen. The cursor again is in the blank line between the markers. Type the following reference using `^PU` or Shift-F4 to mark the beginning and end of the underlined text.

`Massone, Elbert and Eva Jensen. "`<u>`Employee Responses to Office`</u>
<u>`Automation,`</u>`" Today's Office, 3 (May, 1973), 17-34.`

Press Return twice to insert a blank line between the tags. You want to do this when typing each note so they will be separated by a blank line during printing. When you are done typing the information for the note, move the cursor past the second command marker and continue typing the text of the paper.

This note will be marked on the screen by a highlighted 1. The next reference you type will automatically be numbered 2. Sequential numbering continues through the document.

**Removing an Endnote**—Now let's assume that you want to remove one of the notes you have typed in the document. Move the cursor to the highlighted number marking the location of the note. Turn the display on by typing

`^OD`

or by pressing Shift-F1. Like a header or footer, to remove the endnote, simply remove all of the text between the markers. The markers disappear when the text is gone, and WordStar 2000 automatically renumbers all endnotes that follow.

**Adding an Endnote**—You may also add some text within an existing paragraph and consequently need to add another endnote reference. You don't need to be concerned about what this endnote's number is. Simply use the command `^ON` and type the text. WordStar 2000 automatically assigns the new note the appropriate sequential number and continues through the document renumbering the remaining notes.

**Changing an Endnote**—Making changes in an existing endnote is easy. You move the cursor to the endnote and turn the display on with `^OD` or Shift-F1. Move the cursor into the area between the command markers and make the necessary changes. When you move the cursor past the command markers you can continue typing or editing the rest of the document.

**Moving the Cursor Through Endnotes**—You can also move the cursor through the document, jumping from note to note or leaping the cursor to a specific note number. To do this, type

`^CN`

for Cursor Note. WordStar 2000 prompts

```
Go to which footnote number?
(Press + for next footnote or - for last)
```

If you type a number and press Return, WordStar 2000 moves the cursor to the requested note. To move the cursor to the next note reference, press the plus key.

To move the cursor to the previous note, press either the minus or hyphen key.

This command also lets you move ahead or back a specified number of notes. For example, if you are on note 3 and want to go to note 6, you can type +3 and press Return to move forward three notes. Likewise, if you are at note 6 and want to move to note 3, you would type −3 and press Return.

**When Endnotes Print**—When you print the document, WordStar 2000 prints all of the notes at the end of the document. The references within the text are made with superscripted numbers that match the highlighted numbers you see in the text.

The endnotes at the end of the document print in numbered sequence. When you typed the text of the endnotes in the document, you pressed Return twice at the end of each. Inserting this blank line causes them to print separated by a blank line.

You will also want the endnotes to print beginning a new page at the end of the document. So following the last page of the text, give the command that begins a new page

`^OP`

**Format of Endnotes**—The format of the endnotes can also be different from the rest of the document. For example, you might want them to print using different margins. The research paper format specifies that the document must have a right margin of 60. Let's say that you want the endnotes to print using a right margin of 50.

You can specify this is one of two ways. First, you could include the right margin command when you type the text for the first note. WordStar 2000 will apply this new Ruler Line to the notes, but not to the text of the document.

The second way is to change the right margin at the end of the document. Because the command is given at the end, the text in the paper remains unchanged. However, the endnotes print following the last page of the text, so the new Ruler Line will be used for formatting the notes.

## TYPING FOOTNOTES

Unlike the endnotes—remember that WordStar 2000 calls them *footnotes*—discussed in the previous section, true footnotes that print at the bottom of the page are done manually. WordStar 2000 performs no computer magic on them. It is up to you to type the superscripted reference numbers and change them if you add and delete references.

Let's return to the example used earlier to illustrate endnotes. Let's say that you just typed this sentence in your paper.

```
Although little research has been done to study the rela-
tionship between the use of word processors and job satis-
faction, literature seems to support the early findings of
Massone and Jensen.
```

Leave the cursor in the space immediately following the period that ends the sentence. Because you are referring specifically to someone else's research, you need to mark it with a superscript 1 to identify that it has a footnote. You'll type the footnote at the bottom of the page.

Do you recall the superscript command? Type

```
^P+
```

using either the plus that shares the equal key (remember to use the Shift key) or the plus on the numeric keypad. Type

```
1
```

which is the number of the footnote. Then give the superscript command again by typing

```
^P+
```

to return printing to the normal line of print.

**Positioning the Footnote**—Placing the footnote text at the bottom of the page is up to you. Let's say that your style guide dictates that an 18-character underline is printed a single space below the last row of text to separate the text from the footnote. The footnote begins a double space below the line. The first line of the footnote is indented eight spaces, is single-spaced and is preceded by a superscripted number.

Notice that some of the format parameters again require single spacing. So after typing the last line of text preceding the footnote, give the line spacing command to change to single spacing. You'll type

```
^PH
```

for Print Height, highlight the 6.00 option and press Return.

If the text including the footnote reference falls at the bottom of the page, the text and footnote will look like this:

```
Although little research has been done to study the rela-
tionship between the use of word processors and job satis-
```

```
faction, literature seems to support the early findings of
Massone and Jensen.¹
```

---------

```
        ¹Massone, Elbert and Eva Jensen. "Employee Re-
sponses to Office Automation," Today's Office, 3 (May,
1973), 17-34.
```

Obviously, not all references will fall neatly at the bottom of the page. Also, a page is not limited to one footnote. You may have two, three or more citations on one page. So what do you do to make it work?

Honestly, it may require some trial and error. You can type the text of the footnotes for the page, mark them as a block and move the block to the bottom of the page shifting lines of text around as necessary until it all fits properly on the page.

Obviously, this isn't a simple solution, but you do have a "fudge factor" that isn't offered by a typewriter. If the footnotes don't fit well when you use WordStar 2000, you can rearrange things until they do fit the way you want them—all without liquid correction fluid and eraser crumbs!

**An Alternative to Footnotes**—Another format for citing references is commonly acceptable. Rather than using footnotes, consider using the bibliographic entries at the end of the paper as citations. Number each entry in the bibliography. Then in the paper, make references to a particular publication simply by listing the number of the publication.

For example, you might type

```
(20, 21, 24-26)
```

including the parentheses to make reference to these five publications. To obtain further details about these citations, the reader turns to the numerically ordered bibliography for the details. This is certainly easier than making five endnotes or five footnotes at the bottom of the page to take care of these five publications.

## TYPING THE BIBLIOGRAPHY

The previous chapter illustrated the bibliographic entry as an example of the hanging indent. The first line of the entry begins at the left margin and each of the remaining lines of the entry is indented to a tab setting.

Let's use the examples from the previous chapter to look at several ways of putting them in order. Notice that the format of the entries has changed slightly. Because our research paper style requires an eight-character paragraph indent, the second line of each bibliographical entry is also indented eight characters. This happened automatically because the indent moves to the first tab setting when the format of the document is changed. The previous format for the bibliographic entries had tabs set every five columns. The current format has tabs set every eight columns.

```
Adrian, Vivienne. The Wonderful World of Word Processing.
        Helena, MT:Excellent Press, 1984. 164 pp.
Type, Tella. Developing a Way With Words. Springfield, IL:
        Tella Publishing, 64 pp.
Zorta, Tim. The Art of Biography Writing. Nowata,
        OK:Delmar and Sons, Inc., 1983. 256 pp.
```

**Sorting a Numbered List**—Currently, the bibliography is in alphabetic order, a standard and useful way to organize it. However, let's assume now that you are using the number method to refer to publications in the bibliography. When you number the list, it looks like this:

```
3. Adrian, Vivienne. The Wonderful World of Word
        Processing. Helena, MT:Excellent Press, 1984. 164
        pp.
1. Type, Tella. Developing a Way With Words. Springfield,
        IL:Tella Publishing, 64 pp.
2. Zorta, Tim. The Art of Biography Writing. Nowata,
        OK:Delmar and Sons, Inc., 1983. 256 pp.
```

You need a quick way to put them in numeric order. You can do this with WordStar 2000's sort feature.

First, set the right margin wide at 150 so each entry will fit on one line. After sorting, you will remove this unwanted Ruler Line and the hanging indent format will return. Position the cursor above the first entry and give the right margin command

```
^TR
```

or Shift-F7. Type

```
150
```

for the column number and press Return.

**Marking a Vertical Block**—You now need to mark a block that includes only the number rather than the entire line of text. This is a *vertical block*. The other blocks you have marked were *horizontal blocks*. When the vertical block is marked, the entries can be sorted numerically. Before marking a vertical block you need to turn the vertical block feature on by typing

```
^BV
```

for Block Vertical. Position the cursor in column 1 of the line with the first entry. Mark the block using the commands you're already familiar with. Type

```
^BB
```

or simply press F9 to mark the beginning. Now move the cursor to column 2 of the line with the last entry. Give the block end command by typing

```
^BE
```

or Shift-F9. The number of each entry is now highlighted.

Note that your version of WordStar 2000 may not let you move the cursor to the far left side of the screen after you have marked the beginning of the vertical block. However, if you position the cursor using the Status Line information at the top of the screen, the block will be properly marked.

**Sorting a Vertical Block**—WordStar 2000 boasts a sorting feature that makes your work easy at a time like this. Type

`^BS`

for Block Sort. WordStar 2000 then prompts

```
Sort Orders:
Ascending     Descending
```

Because the block is to be sorted from 1 to 3, type

`A`

for Ascending. In a few moments WordStar 2000 has rearranged the lines for you.

WordStar 2000 will sort up to 150 lines in one operation, generally quite adequate to care for your bibliography.

**Sorting a List into Alphabetic Order**—To see an alphabetic sort work, remove the numbers from the entries, mark the column block to include the first letter of the author's last name. Give the Block Sort command, `^BS`, and select the ascending order again.

**Bring Back the Indents**—Because the entries are now sorted alphabetically (or numeric if you skipped the last step) as you want them, you can remove the Ruler Line that set the right margin at 150. To do this, turn the display on by typing

`^OD`

or Shift-F1. Position the cursor on the line and remove it by typing

`^RE`

or pressing Shift-F6. Immediately, the entries shift, putting the hanging indents back in effect if you originally included them in the entries.

## SPECIAL CHALLENGES

Most research papers also include other challenges for you and WordStar 2000—tables, superscripts and subscripts, extra-wide text and tables and more. However, most of these are also frequent ingredients in reports, here defined as being more general and less specialized documents. These tasks are discussed in the next chapter.

# 11 Writing A Report

The previous chapter introduced you to the fine points of writing a research paper requiring a special format. We used the example of preparing a thesis. This chapter continues with more features that you might need for preparing such a special research paper or a more general report. These include procedures for creating and rearranging tables, printing superscripts and subscripts, and setting up formulas.

StarIndex, one of the components of the WordStar 2000 Plus package, is also useful for adding the final touches to a report—the table of contents and an index. Using StarIndex is in Part III of this book.

## CREATING TABLES

Tables are columns and rows of information. Tables are frequently used in reports because they present a lot of information in an easy-to-use format. For example, tables may summarize monthly sales comparisons for a corporation for the past three years, state the raw data for individual physical-fitness tests, or provide a list of pertinent employee information. Tables may be a few lines long or span several pages. They may be relatively simple with only two columns or may stretch to 10 or more columns wide.

Whatever the information the table communicates and regardless of its size, you need to be able to quickly set up a table. With WordStar 2000 you can just as quickly rearrange the columns if you need to present the information in a different format or if you typed it incorrectly the first time. Once the information is typed, you can use the column block feature to mark and move or copy columns to other locations. Or, if the column is no longer needed, you can easily remove it, letting the other columns shift to fill in the space. You can also use the Block Sort command to reorder the lines in the columns.

This chapter illustrates the procedure for setting up columns and tables that are non-calculative. In other words, they report information but don't require totals, averages or other calculations to be performed on them. The next chapter shows you how to use the built-in math capabilities of WordStar 2000 to perform calculations on numbers in a table.

## TABLE FORMAT

Preparing a table is a two-fold process. First, you need to plan the design or format. What will the margins be? Will it be double- or single-spaced? Where will the tabs be set? Second, you do the actual typing of the information into the format you have created.

Let's create a TABLE.FRM format. Type

F

from the Opening Menu. Specify 10 pitch type, single spacing, right margin at 70, no tabs, and ragged-right lines. To omit all tab settings from the format, type

0

when WordStar 2000 prompts for the tab interval.

We are assuming that the only thing in our document is a table. For this reason, the format was designed specifically to meet the needs of the table. Later we'll look at the changes you would make to type a table surrounded by text.
**Table Document**—Now create a document named TABLE using the TABLE.FRM format. Notice that the Ruler Line at the top of the screen shows the left and right margins, but there are no inverted triangles showing tabs. This is because tabs were not specified in the TABLE.FRM format design.

Let's say that you need to type and print a list of the employees in the business office, their job titles, current salaries, and years of experience. Here is the table as you will initially type it:

BUSINESS OFFICE PERSONNEL

| EMPLOYEE | TITLE | SALARY | YRS. EXPERIENCE |
|---|---|---|---|
| Kennedy, Pam | Senior Clerk | $10,530 | 4 |
| Adrian, Ed | Senior Clerk | 10,200 | 3 |
| Barnett, Betty | Supervisor 1 | 15,850 | 7 |
| Tyler, Trina | Accountant 2 | 22,510 | 2 |
| Cardin, Arlen | Manager 3 | 18,320 | 5 |
| Edwin, Ava | Secretary | 11,305 | 6 |
| Amil, Lou | Clerk | 9,890 | 1 |
| Frank, Ardyth | Clerk | 8,245 | 2 |
| Garvey, Erin | Director | 28,480 | 6 |

Type the table heading

`BUSINESS OFFICE PERSONNEL`

and center it by typing

`^OC`

or pressing Shift-F2. Now type the column headings. With the cursor in column 1, type

`EMPLOYEE`

Then press the Spacebar to move the cursor to column 23 where you type

`TITLE`

Again, press the Spacebar to move the cursor to column 41 and type

`SALARY`

Finally, move the cursor to column 51 and type

`YRS. EXPERIENCE`

If, after typing the columns of information, you see that the headings are not aligned as you want them, you can easily add and delete spaces to move them.
**Setting Tabs** — To make typing the information under the column headings easier, you need to set tabs. In fact, to guarantee that columns will be properly aligned, you need to use tabs to move from column to column. Pressing the Spacebar does not assure that the columns will be lined up during printing. This is particularly true if you are using a proportional font because WordStar 2000 would adjust the size of the spaces inserted with the Spacebar.

The *EMPLOYEE* column is typed beginning at the left margin so no tab is required for it. However, you will set a tab to align the other three columns.

To type the information in the *TITLE* column, you will set a tab in column 22. To do this, type

`^TS`

for Tab Set or press F8. WordStar 2000 then asks

`Set tab in what column?`

and you type

`22`

and press Return. An inverted triangle appears on the Ruler Line. The first character of each of the items in this column will align in column 22.
**Setting Decimal Tabs** — The *SALARY* column contains dollar amounts that need to be aligned on the right. To have WordStar 2000 do this for you automatically, you will set a decimal tab in column 46, the position of the last number. Although the numbers in this column do not contain a decimal, WordStar 2000 will align the numbers as though a decimal point follows.

To set a decimal tab, type

^TD

for Tab Decimal. When WordStar 2000 asks

Decimal tab in what column?

type

46

and press Return.

Using a decimal tab makes alignment easier than typing columns with the familiar typewriter method. Using the typewriter, you tabbed to the tab setting and spaced forward or backward as necessary to align the numbers. However, decimal tabs make WordStar 2000 responsible for keeping the numbers in place and aligned.

The last tab you will set is for typing the *YRS. EXPERIENCE* in column 58. Because the numbers in this column are each one digit, you can set a regular tab to align them. If, however, some of the employees had 10 or more years of experience requiring two digits, you might again set a decimal tab to align the numbers on the right.

Give the Tab Set command again by typing

^TS

or by pressing F8 and typing

58

followed by Return.

Now the table tab format and headings are complete. You are ready to type the information.

**Typing Columns**—Now type the names and other information as you saw them earlier. After typing the name, press the Tab key to move to the next column to type the job title. Then tab again to type the salary and press tab a final time to type the number of years of experience. Press Return to move the cursor to the next line and type the information for the next employee. Continue until all of the information is put in.

**Sorting the Table Alphabetically**—You will notice that the information is not currently in any order. The employees are not in alphabetical order—neither is there any recognizable sequence in the other columns. To make the information more useful, let's say that you would like the employee column in alphabetical order. You'll use the Block Sort feature you learned in an earlier chapter.

Let's review the procedure. First, you need to tell WordStar 2000 that you want to mark a column block. You recall that you type

^BV

for Block Vertical. The column you will mark is the first letter of the last names of the employees. Move the cursor to the *K* of Pam Kennedy's last name and give the Begin Block command

^BB

or press F9. Then move the cursor down to mark the end of the block. Put the cursor in column 2 on Erin Garvey's line and give the Block End command

^BE

or Shift-F9.

The first letter of each employee's last name is now highlighted. To put the list in alphabetical order, give the Block Sort command by typing

^BS

and type

A

to tell WordStar 2000 you want to sort it in ascending order, that is, from A to Z. In just a moment you see the entire list rearranged! Notice now that WordStar 2000 rearranged the entire line during the sort so each employee is still matched with his or her correct job title, salary and experience.

This is the newly sorted table:

BUSINESS OFFICE PERSONNEL

| EMPLOYEE | TITLE | SALARY | YRS. EXPERIENCE |
|---|---|---|---|
| Adrian, Ed | Senior Clerk | 10,200 | 3 |
| Amil, Lou | Clerk | 9,890 | 1 |
| Barnett, Betty | Supervisor 1 | 15,850 | 7 |
| Cardin, Arlen | Manager 3 | 18,320 | 5 |
| Edwin, Ava | Secretary | 11,305 | 6 |
| Frank, Ardyth | Clerk | 8,245 | 2 |
| Garvey, Erin | Director | 28,480 | 6 |
| Kennedy, Pam | Senior Clerk | $10,530 | 4 |
| Tyler, Trina | Accountant 2 | 22,510 | 2 |

The only thing slightly out of place is the *$* in the salary column. Delete it from Pam Kennedy's line and type it on the first line of the column.

**Sorting Another Column**—You can sort any column you choose in the table. It does not need to be the first one. You could sort the experience column to put the employees in a seniority order. Or, you could have the table ordered by salary.

Let's sort the title column into alphabetical order. Again, the block needs to be marked. The Vertical Block feature should still be in effect from the previous block sort exercise. If it is you see `Vert` in the upper-right part of the screen. Type

`^BV`

if you see `Horiz` on the top line.

Now let's mark the block in the *TITLE* column. You will include the first three characters of the title in the block, so it will sort correctly. If only the first character is included, the three titles beginning with *S* will not sort alphabetically.

Put the cursor on the first letter of Ed Adrian's title and give the Begin Block command

`^BB`

or F9. Then move the cursor to the fourth character of the last person's title and mark the end of the block by typing

`^BE`

or pressing Shift-F9. Again, the first three letters of each person's title is highlighted.

Give the sort command

`^BS`

and type

A

for an Ascending sort. In just a moment WordStar 2000 has again rearranged the table putting the title column in alphabetical order. Again, the dollar sign in the salary column needs to be moved to the first employee's line.

BUSINESS OFFICE PERSONNEL

| EMPLOYEE | TITLE | SALARY | YRS. EXPERIENCE |
|---|---|---|---|
| Tyler, Trina | Accountant 2 | 22,510 | 2 |
| Amil, Lou | Clerk | 9,890 | 1 |
| Frank, Ardyth | Clerk | 8,245 | 2 |
| Garvey, Erin | Director | 28,480 | 6 |
| Cardin, Arlen | Manager 3 | 18,320 | 5 |
| Edwin, Ava | Secretary | 11,305 | 6 |
| Kennedy, Pam | Senior Clerk | 10,530 | 4 |
| Adrian, Ed | Senior Clerk | $10,200 | 3 |
| Barnett, Betty | Supervisor 1 | 15,850 | 7 |

**Moving Columns**—Because the job titles are now in alphabetical order, the table will be more useful if the columns are rearranged, putting the job title column first. You can move this column to put it first. You will mark the TITLE column as a vertical block and move it to the left side of the table.

Because you just finished marking a column block and sorting it, the column feature should still be turned on, so you're ready to mark another column as a block. Place the cursor in column 22 preceding the word *TITLE* heading the column. Give the begin block command

^BB

or F9.

To mark the end of the block, put the cursor in column 40 on the last row of the table. Type the Block End command

^BE

or press Shift-F9. When specifying a column block, you mark the upper-left corner and the lower-right corner of the block. WordStar 2000 then forms a rectangle using the two points you marked. Everything within the rectangle is marked and the entire column is highlighted. The position of the block markers for the column is shown below. Remember that these symbols won't actually stay on your screen. Rather the entire block will be highlighted:

```
                     BUSINESS OFFICE PERSONNEL

    EMPLOYEE             <B>TITLE            SALARY     YRS. EXPERIENCE

    Tyler, Trina        Accountant 2       $22,510          2
    Amil, Lou           Clerk                9,890          1
    Frank, Ardyth       Clerk                8,245          2
    Garvey, Erin        Director            28,480          6
    Cardin, Arlen       Manager 3           18,320          5
    Edwin, Ava          Secretary           11,305          6
    Kennedy, Pam        Senior Clerk        10,530          4
    Adrian, Ed          Senior Clerk        10,200    ·      3
    Barnett, Betty      Supervisor 1     <E>15,850          7
```

Now put the cursor at the place where the upper-left corner of the marked block is to appear when moved. In this case, you will put the cursor on the *E* of *EMPLOYEE* to move the marked column in front of the current first column.

When the cursor is in place, give the Block Move command

^BM

or F10. In just a moment WordStar 2000 rearranges the columns as shown here:

```
                    BUSINESS OFFICE PERSONNEL

     TITLE               EMPLOYEE        SALARY    YRS. EXPERIENCE

     Accountant 2        Tyler, Trina    $22,510        2
     Clerk               Amil, Lou         9,890        1
     Clerk               Frank, Ardyth     8,245        2
     Director            Garvey, Erin     28,480        6
     Manager 3           Cardin, Arlen    18,320        5
     Secretary           Edwin, Ava       11,305        6
     Senior Clerk        Kennedy, Pam     10,530        4
     Senior Clerk        Adrian, Ed       10,200        3
     Supervisor 1        Barnett, Betty   15,850        7
```

**Fixing Minor Problems**—Sometimes when moving columns, a few lines may not be precisely realigned. After moving this column you may find that the dollar sign has attached itself to the wrong column. If some lines seem to be pushed over too far with entries appearing in the wrong column, you can go back to fix them. These minor discrepancies may occur due to blank spaces that were part of the column, and the placement of the tabs and the block markers.

**Underlining Column Headings**—You might want to underline each of the column headings to add a finishing touch to the table. Where you will place the underline commands depends on the format you set up for the table document.

Remember that when you mark text for underlining, you must give the command at the beginning and the end of the text that is to be underlined. The command is turned on and turned off. What will happen if you give the underline command at the beginning and end of the line with the column headings if the document format specifies underlining the spaces between words? You can quickly see that one long continuous underline would be printed like this:

```
     TITLE       EMPLOYEE                    SALARY      YRS. EXPERIENCE
```

This is not necessarily what you want. You might rather prefer that each of the headings be underlined individually. To remedy the situation, you could change the document format to underline only words.

A better choice might be to give the underline command in pairs for each heading. For example, you will type

^PU

for Print Underline or press Shift-F4 before the word *TITLE* and after it. Do the same thing for *EMPLOYEE, SALARY* and *YRS. EXPERIENCE* headings. This will print a continuous underline below the words and spaces within each heading but will not connect all of the headings with a solid line:

```
TITLE        EMPLOYEE                           SALARY      YRS. EXPERIENCE
```

**Copying Column Blocks** — The example just completed showed you how to mark and *move* a column. You can also mark a column and *copy* it by repositioning the cursor and typing

^BC

for Block Copy or by pressing Shift-F10. Remember too that you can copy blocks from one window to another. If you created some information that you want to copy to another section of the same document or copy to a different document, put the text in separate windows and copy the block.

**Deleting Column Blocks** — When a column is no longer needed, you can mark it and delete it using the Block Remove command, ^BR or ^RB. Either of these commands removes a marked block. The block can be either a text block which stretches margin to margin or a column block.

**Table Surrounded by Text** — The example table you typed was assumed to be the only thing in the file. However, sometimes the table appears within text. If it is a short table, it may not be printed on a separate page — it runs in with the rest of the document. When this occurs, you might find it necessary to change tabs before and after the table to format both the table and the text correctly.

**Keep Command** — In addition to maintaining the proper format, you may want to control the occurrence of the page break. Unless the table is more than one page long, you will usually want to be sure that a page break does not fall in the midst of the table. WordStar 2000's Keep command is used to keep or weld a specified number of lines together. These lines can not be separated by a page break unless the command is removed.

Let's use the table you typed as an example. You can require the 13 lines to print on the same page. To do this, place the cursor at the beginning of the line preceding the *BUSINESS OFFICE PERSONNEL* heading. Then type

^OK

for Option Keep. WordStar 2000 asks

How many lines to keep together?

Because the table is 13 lines long, type

13

and press Return. WordStar 2000 inserts the following code at this point

[KEEP NEXT 13 LINES TOGETHER]

You can see the code if you give the Option Display command, ^OD or Shift-F1. When calculating the page breaks, WordStar 2000 reads the code and counts the number of lines remaining on the current page. If there are 13 or more lines, the table falls in behind the preceding text.

However, if there are fewer than 13 lines left on the current page, WordStar 2000 inserts a page break at the point of the Keep command. The entire table then moves to the beginning of the next page.

In this example, when the table moves to the top of the next page, the current page may be up to 12 lines short. You may want to move several lines of text that follow the table to fill the blank lines immediately preceding the table. Keep in mind that WordStar 2000 displays the page breaks on the screen exactly as they will print. This makes it possible for you to manipulate the text on the screen until it appears just as you want it to print.

## TOO WIDE TABLES

At some time you may need to prepare a table that is wider than the normal margins. In fact, it may also be too wide to print on the paper. When this happens, you can make a number of changes that may make it possible to fit the table onto the page.

**Changing Margins**—One of the most obvious solutions to working with a wide table is to extend the right margin. If you need space for only a few more characters, this is an acceptable alternative. Remember though that you won't want the right margin extending past the edge of the paper.

**Changing Page Offset**—Each time you design a format, WordStar 2000 asks for the even and odd page offset. You'll recall that the page offset is a space reserved by WordStar 2000 on the left edge of the paper. Although the left margin of your document is set at 1, printing does not begin at the left edge of the paper if there is an offset.

The page offset affects the entire document because it is included in the format design. It cannot be set from within the document. Changing the page offset to fit long lines on a page works best when the document contains only a table, in other words, when the entire document can share the same offset.

With some manipulation, you may be able to achieve the desired result of varying the page offset throughout the document. To do this, set the page offset to the smallest number you will want to use anywhere in the document when designing the format. Then to increase the size of the page offset for the text, increase the size of the left margin using the left margin commands, ^TL or F7.

Let's look at more specifics for doing this. The default page offset in the format is 10 spaces. If you need more room to fit a table on a page, you can change this to a smaller number like 5. This assumes that the exact size of the left margin is not critical on the printed page.

**Left Margin and Page Offset**—The page offset of 5 sets the format for the table but may not be what you want for the rest of the text. To begin printing the text at the place a 10-space page offset would print, change the left margin to 5. A left margin of 5 plus the 5-space page offset puts the beginning of the line in column 10, the same result produced by a page offset of 10.

When you change the left margin to 5, also extend the right margin by 5. For example, if the margins are currently set at 1 and 65, when the left margin becomes 5, change the right margin to 70. This will give you the same 65-character line.

**The Table**—Let's assume that you now want to fit a wide table within the text. At the point where the table is to start, change the left margin to 1. This means that the table begins printing 5 characters to the left of the preceding text. The right margin is still set at 70, making the lines for the table longer than the ones of the surrounding text.

After typing the table, again set the left margin at 5 and continue with the text.

**Changing Font Size**—Another option available to squeeze more characters on each line is to change the size of the characters. The font choices—typefaces and sizes—are dependent on the printer you selected during installation. You can see the list of options available on the installed printer by typing

^PF

for Print Font.

For example, if you are using a dot matrix printer, your choices may include 12, 15 or 17 characters per inch (cpi). The default is 10 cpi. So you can quickly see that if you reduce the size of each character, you can fit more characters into the same number of inches across the page.

If you change the font size, you may want to print a sample to determine how the page offset, tabs or margins were affected by the character size change. This is the personnel table you typed earlier expanded to include more columns and printed on a dot matrix printer using 17 characters per inch.

BUSINESS OFFICE PERSONNEL

| TITLE | EMPLOYEE | SALARY | YRS. EXPERIENCE | ACCT. | JOB CODE | EDUCATION |
|---|---|---|---|---|---|---|
| Accountant 2 | Tyler, Trina | $22,510 | 2 | 86317 | 18 | BA |
| Clerk | Amil, Lou | 9,890 | 1 | 86316 | 8 | HS |
| Clerk | Frank, Ardyth | 8,245 | 2 | 86316 | 8 | HS |
| Director | Garvey, Erin | 28,480 | 6 | 86320 | 32 | MS+12 |
| Manager 3 | Cardin, Arlen | 18,320 | 5 | 86319 | 25 | BS |
| Secretary | Edwin, Ava | 11,305 | 6 | 86320 | 15 | 2 YRS |
| Senior Clerk | Kennedy, Pam | 10,530 | 4 | 86316 | 12 | 2 YRS |
| Senior Clerk | Adrian, Ed | 10,200 | 3 | 86316 | 12 | 1 YR |
| Supervisor 1 | Barnett, Betty | 15,850 | 7 | 86319 | 15 | BA |

**Proportional Spacing**—One of the options offered by many letter-quality printers is proportional spacing, which permits WordStar 2000 to adjust the amount of space allocated to different characters. Wide characters such as *m* and *W* get more space; narrow characters such as *l* and *i* get less.

As mentioned earlier in this chapter, if you selected a proportional font while designing the format or after typing ^PF, you must be certain to press the Tab key to move the cursor from column to column. If you press the Spacebar, WordStar 2000 will adjust the size of the spaces. The result will be poorly aligned columns.

When using a proportional font, you may also notice that the column number on the Status Line does not change every time you type a character. This is because WordStar 2000 is calculating the amount of space used by each character you type. If several narrow characters appear together in a word, they will not each take up one column as tallied by the number at the top of the screen or window. For example, a short word like *ill*, comprised of narrow characters, may fit into two columns of space.

**Changing Paper Size**—If these changes won't fit the table on the page, you can change the position of the paper. In other words, you might roll the wide edge of the paper into the printer first if the printer is wide enough to accommodate this. The result is a page 11 inches wide and 8-1/2 high, assuming that you are using standard paper. When using a different width paper, remember to change the right margin so you can take advantage of the additional width. At the same time you should change the page length.

A page 11 inches wide could print 110 characters if you set 10 cpi. To allow an inch margin on the left and right, you could set the left margin at 1, the right margin at 90, and the page offset at 10.

When the right margin is set wider than the 80 characters that can be displayed on the screen at one time, the text will scroll sideways. This is very similar to the text scrolling up and down to display different parts of the document, which you are already familiar with.

**Changing Page Length**—If you change the paper size or insert the paper into the printer another way, be sure to adjust the page length as well. This can only be done in the document format where the page length is specified in lines.

For example, a standard 11-inch page has 66 single-spaced lines. However, when you turn the paper to insert it into the printer, the length is 8-1/2 inches. With 6 lines per inch, the page length is 51 lines.

You cannot mix different page lengths within a WordStar 2000 document. This means that if you need to print a page on a different length paper you need to put that table or portion of the document in a separate file with a format designed to meet its needs.

## FORMULAS

Formulas are also common components of reports. These might be simple equations with superscripts like the Pythagorean theorem: $A^2 + B^2 = C^2$. Or they may become very complex like this hypothetical formula:

$$\dfrac{\dfrac{[(a^2+b^2)-(v_{max}-b)^{(r+1)^2}]}{R_x + A(v+b)}}{.076(B^2-(a+b))}$$

**Typing the Formula**—Because WordStar 2000 does a pretty good job of showing you the text on the screen the way it will print, you can type each part of the formula at the place you want it to be. Superscripts—raised characters—and subscripts—lowered characters—present some special challenges in the creation of formulas.

**Typing Superscripts and Subscripts**—Generally, superscripts and subscripts are printed a half space above or below the line of print. As you learned in earlier chapters, you can give the superscript and subscript commands that will print the characters in place on paper. They are not displayed in their raised and lowered positions on the screen, however. The command for the superscript is

^P+

and the subscript is

^P−

Remember to give them in pairs—once to turn the feature on and again to turn it off. The ^P+ and ^P− commands will usually meet your needs. The sample formula illustrated earlier, however, has a double superscript at the end of the first line.

The $(r+1)$ is a superscript, and the 2 is superscripted above it. To print the 2 in place, you will need to put the cursor in the line above.

**Changing Line Spacing**—Perhaps the ideal way to get these notations typed in place without giving any special commands would be to change the line spacing to one-half. Unfortunately, this isn't one of the options offered by WordStar 2000. You can get no closer than eight lines per inch, which is three-quarter spacing.

To change the line spacing, position the cursor where you want to type the formula. Then type

`^PH`

for Print Height. Move the highlight bar to 8.00 and press Return. Then type the formula, literally positioning each character where it will print without using superscript and subscript commands. The formula shown earlier was printed with a letter-quality printer using the 8.00 line spacing. If the formula is in the midst of a document, you will need to change the line spacing back to the earlier setting when the typing is finished.

The next chapter continues discussion of columns. The difference will be that the columns are numeric. You will perform calculations on the columns, allowing you to explore the math capabilities of WordStar 2000.

# 12 Preparing Numeric Reports & Using Math

This chapter discusses further work with columns using WordStar 2000's math capabilities. The columns designed in the previous chapter stated information and gave facts. However, you made no attempt to calculate the total salary expenditures for the business office. Nor did you calculate average salaries by job title, category or experience. This chapter will show you how to use the convenient math capabilities of WordStar 2000 to make such calculations.

A word processor is not usually the kind of program used to turn your computer into a calculator. Generally, this is the task of an *electronic spreadsheet,* which is specifically designed to add, subtract, multiply and divide columns and rows of figures. However, because numbers are so often included in documents you prepare, the math capabilities available in WordStar 2000 let you quickly add a column of numbers or extend prices in an invoice without the assistance of a calculator or spreadsheet.

You will find many uses for the math features. You can easily prepare your monthly treasurer's report summarizing receipts and expenses for your club. When you write a letter explaining a discrepancy in a bill you received, you can add and subtract figures or calculate a discount percentage while you write. Invoices for your small home business or a hobby can be typed and calculated—all with a word processor.

Keep in mind that the calculation capabilities of WordStar 2000 are not designed to challenge the complex formula executions of popular spreadsheet programs. However, for your relatively simple tasks, WordStar 2000 can be very convenient.

## MATH WITH WORDSTAR 2000

WordStar 2000 can perform five basic math functions for you—addition, subtraction, multiplication, division and exponentiation. Symbols tell WordStar 2000 what kinds of calculations will take place and in what order. The figures you want to have calculated are marked as a block, either vertical or horizontal. Position the cursor where you want the total to print. Then give the Block Arithmetic command—^BA—to let WordStar 2000 do the calculation. Numbers to be calculated and the totals can be up to 13 digits long, including a decimal point.

## ADDITION

WordStar 2000 assumes that the numbers in the block are to be added unless you indicate otherwise. To specify other calculations, you will use standard mathematical notation explained a little later.

To take a look at WordStar 2000's addition feature, let's say that you want to add these two numbers

```
$ 621.88
  123.45
$
```

You need to mark the numbers as a column block using the following familiar commands:

^BV for Block Vertical to turn on the column feature.

^BB or F9 with the cursor positioned at the upper-left corner of the block.

^BE or Shift-F9 with the cursor positioned at the lower-right corner of the block.

When the block is marked, position the cursor after the dollar sign where you want the total to appear. Then you type another block command

^BA

for Block Arithmetic. Almost instantly the sum appears on the screen beginning at the cursor's position.

```
$621.88
 123.45
$745.33
```

Notice that WordStar 2000 does not require decimal points to be aligned vertically. In fact, the numbers don't need to be vertically aligned or even next to each other. The numbers can be anywhere in the block. In other words, WordStar 2000 can add numbers within sequential text, such as the following sentence, if you can include them in a marked block:

```
The $621.88 payment secures your reservation on the Alaskan
tour. The additional amount of $123.45 must be paid within
fifteen days of the departure. This makes the tour total price
$ .
```

Mark the paragraph as a block—you'll need to turn off the vertical block if you followed the previous example. Then position the cursor immediately after the final dollar sign, and give the Block Arithmetic command

```
^BA
```

Any words, commas, dollar signs or other non-mathematical punctuation (more on these throughout the chapter) are ignored by WordStar 2000 during its calculation.

**Symbols for Addition**—As stated, WordStar 2000 assumes that numbers are to be added unless another indication is given. Sometimes, though, you may want to include a symbol that will also print in the document. The symbol for addition—as you might guess—is the plus sign, +. For example, you might want to include this symbol to make the example shown earlier clearer to the reader.

```
$ 621.88
+ 123.45
$ 745.33
```

In this example, the result of performing arithmetic on the block will be the same with or without the plus sign.

**Spacing For Addition**—You can also type numbers horizontally separated by only a space. WordStar 2000 can then add them. Let's say you are hurriedly typing a document and need to get the total for five numbers. The total will be included in the document; the five numbers will not.

In a blank part of the document, type the five numbers

```
25 381 260 78 84
```

Although you could type the plus sign between the numbers, it is not required. And if you're really in a hurry, you won't want to! Mark the numbers as a block, put the cursor where the total is to appear and give the Block Arithmetic command—^BA. When the total appears, you can delete your "scratch" line.

**Using Windows**—A blank window would seem to be a convenient place for such a "scratch pad." However, WordStar 2000 is not capable of calculating in one window and inserting a total in another. For example, let's say you typed the numbers above in a second window, marked them as a block, then moved the cursor to the first window to mark the place where the total is to print. When you give the Block Arithmetic command, WordStar 2000 calculates the total as 0—not a correct answer.

**Decimal Point Precision**—Decimal points can be part of any number. WordStar 2000 usually includes the decimal point and two digits to the right, even if a decimal point wasn't included in the numbers being added. For example, when you ask WordStar 2000 to add

`4+8`

the answer is 12.00. However, if you add

`4.0 + 8.0`

WordStar 2000's answer is 12.0. The answer will provide as many digits to the right of the decimal point as the most precise number has. For example, when you add

`4 + 8.0 + 12.33 + 3.126`

the answer is 27.456. Three digits to the right of the decimal point are included because one of the numbers added had three.

## SUBTRACTION

Let's use these same numbers arranged in a different way to illustrate WordStar 2000's subtraction capability. Type

```
Total tour price     $ 745.33
Amount paid           -621.88
Balance due          $
```

Mark the numbers as a block, making sure the minus sign is also included in the block. Put the cursor in the second space following the dollar sign on the balance-due line and give the Block Arithmetic command, ^BA. The total, `123.45`, appears almost instantly.

```
Total tour price     $ 745.33
Amount paid           -621.88
Balance due          $ 123.45
```

**Subtraction Symbols**—This time WordStar 2000 knew you wanted to subtract because the minus sign preceded one of the numbers. If you did not type the minus sign (hyphen), WordStar 2000 would have added the numbers, resulting in a total that would disgruntle any tourist!

The minus sign must also be included in the block. If it is not, WordStar 2000 will be unable to locate a math function command and assumes the numbers are to be added.

Brackets are another common way to indicate negative numbers or amounts that are to be subtracted. You'll see this usage in balance sheets or financial reports to identify negative numbers. For example, the calculation shown earlier could be written

```
Total tour price     $ 745.33
Amount paid           <621.88>
Balance due          $
```

Brackets and the minus sign produce the same calculation results. Again, you must include the brackets in the block so WordStar 2000 can calculate it correctly.

**Mixing Addition and Subtraction**—You can also mix addition and subtraction in the same block. There are times when you have a column of numbers that includes both numbers to be added and numbers to be subtracted. For example, you might give a client this summary of the charges for a tour:

```
Base Tour Price          $ 1,099
Air Fare Increase        +    85
1 extra day              +    62
Group travel discount    -   157
Early payment discount   -   100
Total Price              $
```

When you mark the column as a block—be sure to include the plus and minus signs—and give the Block Arithmetic command, WordStar 2000 inserts the total of 989.00.

```
Base Tour Price          $ 1,099
Air Fare Increase        +    85
1 extra day              +    62
Group travel discount    -   157
Early payment discount   -   100
Total Price              $ 989.00
```

Again, you could omit the plus sign before the items to be added because WordStar 2000 automatically assumes addition. In other words, you could have typed the figures like this:

```
Base Tour Price          $ 1,099
Air Fare Increase             85
1 extra day                   62
Group travel discount    -   157
Early payment discount   -   100
Total Price              $ 989.00
```

The result with or without the plus signs will be the same. Another way would be to use the brackets to identify the numbers to be subtracted:

```
Base Tour Price          $ 1,099
Air Fare Increase             85
1 extra day                   62
Group travel discount    < 157 >
Early payment discount   < 100 >
Total Price              $ 989.00
```

As you can see, mixing addition and subtraction—positive and negative numbers—is quick and easy. Actually, only the negative numbers need to be marked, but you might also use the plus sign to help your reader understand the calculations.

## MULTIPLICATION

WordStar 2000 can multiply as easily as it can add and subtract. For example, you will find this useful for extending prices in an itemized invoice. Let's say that you are submitting a reimbursement request to your employer for expenses incurred during a recent business trip. It might include items like this:

```
345 miles @ $.20 per mile
2 nights at La Plaza Hotel @ $52.00
3 days meal allowance @ $35.00
phone calls                                          18.32
        TOTAL                                    $
```

What you need to do is multiply the numbers in each line. You will do this one line at a time. Mark the first line as a block. If necessary type ^BV to turn off the vertical block feature. Then position the cursor to the right of the text line where the total is to print and type

^BA

the Block Arithmetic command. WordStar 2000 then calculates the column. Notice that WordStar 2000 has one command for all math calculations, ^BA. The symbols you include in the block tell WordStar 2000 what kinds of calculations you want performed.

After the first row is calculated, your screen will look like this:

```
345 miles @ $.20 per mile                       69.00
2 nights at La Plaza Hotel @ $52.00
3 days meal allowance @ $35.00
phone calls                                     18.32
        TOTAL                                $
```

Mark the next line as a block and calculate it and then do the third line. When all of the lines have been calculated, your screen will look like this:

```
345 miles @ $.20 per mile                       69.00
2 nights at La Plaza Hotel @ $52.00            104.00
3 days meal allowance @ $35.00                 105.00
phone calls                                     18.32
        TOTAL                                $
```

To finish the reimbursement request, you can add the last column and print the total. You'll need to turn on the column block feature again with ^BV:

```
345 miles @ $.20 per mile                       69.00
2 nights at La Plaza Hotel @ $52.00            104.00
3 days meal allowance @ $35.00                 105.00
phone calls                                     18.32
        TOTAL                             $  296.32
```

**Symbols for Multiplication**—As you saw in the example above, the "at" sign, @, is one of the symbols WordStar 2000 recognizes for multiplication. This is useful because the math symbol can also stay in the text. You don't need to go back to remove it for any reason.

You can also use the asterisk, *, to indicate multiplication. To use the asterisk in the previous example, you might need to word the requisition a bit differently.

| | |
|---|---:|
| 345 miles (345 * $.20 per mile) | 69.00 |
| 2 nights at La Plaza Hotel (2 * $52.00) | 104.00 |
| 3 days meal allowance (3 * $35.00) | 105.00 |
| phone calls | 18.32 |
| TOTAL | $ 296.32 |

In this example, you would include only the numbers enclosed by the parentheses in the block. You would not include the entire line in the block. Do you see why? If you mark the entire first line as a block and give the Block Arithmetic command, WordStar 2000 will multiply 345 by 20 cents just as you wanted. But then it will add 345 to the total. Remember that WordStar 2000 calculates *all* of the numbers in the block. The numbers in parentheses will be multiplied because of the asterisk. The first 345 is then added to the multiplied total because of WordStar 2000's assumption that unmarked numbers are to be added.

## DIVISION

The fourth math function WordStar 2000 performs for you is division. The symbol to identify division is the slash, /. For example, if you type

10/2

WordStar 2000 knows to divide 10 by 2. When you mark the numbers as a block and give the Block Arithmetic command, WordStar 2000 provides the total 5 . 0 0.
**Specifying Order of Calculation**—Unless you specify otherwise, multiplication and division are done before addition and subtraction during math calculations. For example, if you type

3+8*2

WordStar 2000 calculates the total as 19.00. It first multiplies 8 by 2, then adds 3 to that total. It follows the order of multiplication and division first, then addition and subtraction, even though this doesn't follow the order of the numbers and calculation commands as you read them from left to right.

However, you can change WordStar 2000's calculation order. For example, suppose you want to add 3 and 8, then multiply that total by 2. To indicate this to WordStar 2000, you need to use parentheses. The calculations inside the parentheses will be performed first, resulting in a different total, in this case. Note the difference in the totals resulting from the use of parentheses that change the order of calculation.

```
3+8*2   =   19.00
(3+8)*2 =   22.00
```

## EXPONENTIATION

The fifth math function WordStar 2000 performs is *exponentiation*. This means multiplying one number by its *exponent*. Basically, the exponent indicates how many times the number is to be multiplied by itself. You usually see an exponent as a raised number to the right of another number. For example, $2^2$ is the same as saying 2*2. This can also be called *2 to the power of 2, 2 to the second power,* or *2 squared.*

Using the exponent of 3, as in $2^3$ means 2*2*2, multiplying 2 by itself 3 times. This also called *2 to the power of 3, two to the third power,* or *2 cubed.*

**Exponentiation Symbol**—The symbol for exponentiation in WordStar 2000 is the caret, ^. Thus far in the book, the caret symbol is shorthand for the Ctrl Key. However, when dealing with exponentiation, you use the caret "literally." Type Shift-6 to get the caret on the screen. To give the exponentiation command, you do not use the Ctrl Key.

For example, to get the answer for $2^3$ you will type

```
2^3
```

mark it as a block, and type

```
^BA
```

the Block Arithmetic command. The answer is 8.00.

**Exponentiation Limitations**—In all WordStar 2000 math calculations, you must use numbers with fewer than 13 digits. If the calculation you request involves numbers (the answer too) with more characters, you will see asterisks on the screen. For example, if you ask WordStar 2000 to calculate

```
32^81
```

the answer will be

```
* * * * * * * * * * * * *
```

Also, the exponent must be a positive number. For example, asking WordStar 2000 to calculate

```
2^-2
```

produces

```
0
```

for an answer.

**Printing the Superscript Exponent**—If you are printing the equation with an exponent, you want the exponent to be superscript. You can include the superscript command without affecting WordStar 2000's ability to calculate. To print the 3 superscript in $2^3$ you will type the superscript command before and after the 3. You recall that the superscript command is ^P+. In this case the caret indicates the Control key.

## PUTTING IT ALL TOGETHER

Now you know what WordStar 2000's math capabilities are. Type the following table. You will then add the columns and rows to produce totals.

```
                        WELLINGTON TRAVEL

    ITEM              JAN       FEB       MAR      TOTAL      MO AVG

    Rent            500.00    500.00    500.00
    Phone           322.81    240.18    376.02
    Equip Lease     349.21    451.34    475.98
    Travel        1,039.00    312.17    418.66
    Postage          84.17    176.74    214.36

    TOTAL
```

By using the block addition feature, you can calculate rows and columns to give you information for first-quarter, non-salary expenses. WordStar 2000 does not insert the comma into the totals. If you want to use a comma for amounts over 1,000, add them after the total is calculated.

```
                        WELLINGTON TRAVEL

    ITEM            JAN       FEB       MAR      TOTAL      MO AVG

    Rent          500.00    500.00    500.00  1,500.00
    Phone         322.81    240.18    376.02    939.01
    Equip Lease   349.21    451.34    475.98  1,276.53
    Travel      1,039.00    312.17    418.66  1,769.83
    Postage        84.17    176.74    214.36    475.27

    TOTAL       2,295.19  1,680.43  1,985.02  5,960.64
```

**Calculating Averages**—Now let's say that you want to know the average monthly expenditure for each item this quarter. Although WordStar 2000 does not have an automatic "now calculate an average" command, you can accomplish this easily.

Remember that an average is the sum of some numbers divided by the number of items added to create the sum. In other words, each total of a horizontal row can be divided by 3 to provide a monthly average. You could have WordStar 2000 calculate the average month's rent. However, that is not really necessary because each amount was 500.00, so the average must also be 500.00. Simply type

```
500.00
```

in the first line of the *MO AVG* column.

| ITEM | JAN | FEB | MAR | TOTAL | MO AVG |
|------|-----|-----|-----|-------|--------|
| Rent | 500.00 | 500.00 | 500.00 | 1500.00 | 500.00 |

The phone charges varied from month to month, so you can calculate an average by typing /3 after 939.01 to tell WordStar 2000 to divide by 3:

| ITEM | JAN | FEB | MAR | TOTAL | MO AVG |
|------|-----|-----|-----|-------|--------|
| Rent | 500.00 | 500.00 | 500.00 | 1500.00 | 500.00 |
| Phone | 322.81 | 240.18 | 376.02 | 939.01/3 | |

Now mark 939.01/3 as a block. Position the cursor under the 500.00, the previous average in the *MO AVG* column. Give the Block Arithmetic command, ^BA. WordStar 2000 calculates and types out the total. When the total appears, you can remove the /3 you typed to tell WordStar 2000 to divide.

WELLINGTON TRAVEL

| ITEM | JAN | FEB | MAR | TOTAL | MO AVG |
|------|-----|-----|-----|-------|--------|
| Rent | 500.00 | 500.00 | 500.00 | 1500.00 | 500.00 |
| Phone | 322.81 | 240.18 | 376.02 | 939.01 | 313.00 |

Mark and average the remaining rows until the calculations are completed. You should get the following:

WELLINGTON TRAVEL

| ITEM | JAN | FEB | MAR | TOTAL | MO AVG |
|------|-----|-----|-----|-------|--------|
| Rent | 500.00 | 500.00 | 500.00 | 1,500.00 | 500.00 |
| Phone | 322.81 | 240.18 | 376.02 | 939.01 | 313.00 |
| Equip Lease | 349.21 | 451.34 | 475.98 | 1,276.53 | 425.51 |
| Travel | 1,039.00 | 312.17 | 418.66 | 1,769.83 | 589.94 |
| Postage | 84.17 | 176.74 | 214.36 | 475.27 | 158.42 |
| TOTAL | 2,295.19 | 1,680.43 | 1,985.02 | 5,960.64 | 1,986.88 |

**Projecting Income Growth**—Now add another row to the bottom of this table to show income figures for this quarter. Type the following line a double space below the current *TOTAL* row.

```
INCOME          7,888.90        10,988.98        12,881.23
```

Calculate the total and average for this row. Your table should now look like this:

```
                    WELLINGTON TRAVEL

    ITEM        JAN       FEB       MAR      TOTAL     MO AVG

    Rent        500.00    500.00    500.00   1,500.00   500.00
    Phone       322.81    240.18    376.02     939.01   313.00
    Equip Lease 349.21    451.34    475.98   1,276.53   425.51
    Travel    1,039.00    312.17    418.66   1,769.83   589.94
    Postage      84.17    176.74    214.36     475.27   158.42

    TOTAL     2,295.19  1,680.43  1,985.02   5,960.64 1,986.88

    INCOME    7,888.90 10,988.98 12,881.23  31,759.11 10,586.37
```

**Multiplying by a Percentage**—Finally, let's assume that you want to project a 10% growth in income during the same quarter next year. To help you with the long-range planning, you need to know what the net amounts will actually be. You can multiply each of the monthly income figures by 1.1 to increase the amount by 10 percent.

First, type

```
NEXT YR
```

in the *ITEM* column a double space below *INCOME* so you have a place to put the result of this calculation.

One way to calculate the new amount is to type *1.1 on the line below the income line. You remember that the asterisk is the symbol for multiplying. Mark the January income figure and the multiplier as a vertical block and give the Block Arithmetic command. Then calculate the total and average.

```
    INCOME    7,888.90 10,988.98 12,881.23  31,759.11 10,586.37
              *1.1      *1.1      *1.1
    NEXT YR   8,677.79 12,087.88 14,169.35  34,935.02 11,645.01
```

Remember that WordStar 2000 does not put in commas. You need to do it. When the calculation is complete, you can remove the line with the *1.1 on it. Move the cursor to the beginning of the line and type

^RR

the Remove Right command. The numbers will be erased, leaving the line blank.
    Finally, the completed table should look like this.

---

WELLINGTON TRAVEL

| ITEM | JAN | FEB | MAR | TOTAL | MO AVG |
|------|-----|-----|-----|-------|--------|
| Rent | 500.00 | 500.00 | 500.00 | 1,500.00 | 500.00 |
| Phone | 322.81 | 240.18 | 376.02 | 939.01 | 313.00 |
| Equip Lease | 349.21 | 451.34 | 475.98 | 1,276.53 | 425.51 |
| Travel | 1,039.00 | 312.17 | 418.66 | 1,769.83 | 589.94 |
| Postage | 84.17 | 176.74 | 214.36 | 475.27 | 158.42 |
| TOTAL | 2,295.19 | 1,680.43 | 1,985.02 | 5,960.64 | 1,986.88 |
| INCOME | 7,888.90 | 10,988.98 | 12,881.23 | 31,759.11 | 10,586.37 |
| NEXT YR | 8,677.79 | 12,087.88 | 14,169.35 | 34,935.02 | 11,645.01 |

---

**In Summary**—You have worked through several examples using WordStar 2000's five math functions. As you discovered, using math is quick and easy. It does not require any complex set-up procedures. If you know how to mark blocks and insert standard math symbols, you can do it!

# 13 Making Newsletters, Camera-Ready Copy & Multiple-Text Columns

Are you now editor of your club or professional organization's newsletter because you have a computer, word processor and printer? If it hasn't happened yet, you may want to prepare yourself for the inevitable! Of course, you could try to keep it a secret, but your nicely prepared letters and reports will soon give you away. When you get the assignment, you can use the ideas in this chapter to help you prepare super-looking newsletters.

However, the suggestions in this chapter aren't limited to newsletters. Perhaps you'd like to add a creative touch to the department's announcement sheet reporting transfers, promotions, seminars, and other news of interest to your fellow employees.

Or maybe you have aspirations of getting into publishing in a small way. You might sell ads for a "swap sheet," so folks can sell their refrigerators, give away kittens and announce yard sales. You'd like to print several columns of ads on each sheet of your tabloid.

Many communities have, or could benefit from, some specialized publications. For example, a paper could cover news and reviews about music events, arts and crafts, or another area of special interest in your area. Whether subscriptions to your production are sold or distribution is free, you want to keep production costs down. That's possible with WordStar 2000. You can type and print the newspaper with it and still achieve a very professional look.

Once you're a "publisher" you might find yourself exploring the market for developing directories of home businesses, a self-guided tour book of the historic district of your city or neighborhood, or a guide to apartments for rent or homes offered for sale by the owner. You might even become a free-lance newsletter production editor for clubs and corporations.

Without disappointing the budding entrepreneurs, the list of part-time business ventures now comes to an end. This isn't the real intent of this chapter. However, I mention these ideas to illustrate some of the many ways you can use your computer, WordStar 2000 and the ideas in this chapter. Your venture may be large or small, for personal pleasure or for profit. Whatever the motivation, WordStar 2000 can help you do a professional job.

What do you need to get any of these jobs done? Not much that you aren't already familiar with. You've already used most of the commands you'll need. This chapter shows how to apply them in different ways.

## USING "CUT AND PASTE"

As you begin design of the text, you need to know what WordStar 2000 can and cannot do. It can print multiple text columns on a page but with some limitations, described a bit later. You may still find it desirable to print the text in long narrow columns, then use a "cut-and-paste" method to place text as you want it on the master page.

**Newsletter Format**—Let's assume that you are designing and typing a newsletter consisting of two columns on a regular 8-1/2 by 11-inch page. These columns differ from the tabs and columns of numbers or information you typed in previous chapters. This time, the columns are made of text. Two or more columns on one page give the publication a newspaper or magazine look.

Before typing, design a format you can use for typing newsletters on this size paper. From the Opening Menu type

F

and name the format

NEWSLTR.FRM

Use a 10-pitch font and single-spacing, 6.00 LPI. For now, accept all the default settings. Respond to the form-feed question as your printer requires. Omit page numbering in this format. Because this newsletter is only one page long, it won't require page numbering.

Now create a document named

NEWS-LET

using the NEWSLTR.FRM format.

**Typing the Newsletter**—When using the "cut-and-paste" method to form two columns on one page, you will type the text in one long slender column. You can control the line breaks, hyphenation and other fine points of the format.

**Setting Margins and Tabs**—Because you want two columns of text on the page, you need to determine the width of each column. The right margin is currently set at 65. If each of the two columns is 30 characters wide with 5 blank spaces between the columns, the text will be nicely spaced on the page within the current margins.

However, for typing the text, the right margin needs to be set to the width of the finished columns. With the cursor at the top of the NEWS-LET document, change the right margin by typing

^TR

or Shift-F7 followed by

30

and press Return.

You will type the entire newsletter with these margins. After typing is complete, you will print the text, then form the two columns on the page by pasting them to another paper.

Also, to indent the paragraphs, set a tab by typing

^TS

or pressing F8, then

3

to set a tab in column 3. When you begin a paragraph, press the Tab key once to move the cursor to the starting point.

**Typing Text—**Let's return to the Wellington Travel office to assist with a newsletter. This is a small, one-page publication to keep clients informed about special rates and tour groups, including reports by people who have recently returned from trips. You see the finished newsletter using an unjustified format in Figure 13-1. For now, type the paragraphs as one long column.

**Hyphenation—**With the automatic hyphenation in the format, words will be hyphenated as you type. Because the lines are short, you will likely also want to add other acceptable hyphenation locations by typing the soft-hyphen command,

^O-

**Centering—**Center each of the headings by typing

^OC

or pressing Shift-F2. When typing is complete, save and print the newsletter.

**Cutting and Pasting—**When printing is done, you will determine the half-way point, trim the paper from the columns and paste them to another sheet.

## PRINTING MULTIPLE COLUMNS WITHOUT "CUT AND PASTE"

The method just described is quite familiar to you if you have created newsletters with a typewriter. You may take a look at the procedures and conclude that WordStar 2000 makes the process only a bit easier. You can, however, have WordStar 2000 print the columns side-by-side on the paper and eliminate cutting and pasting. This method speeds the process because the columns are printed "camera-ready."

However, with this method you can't use some of WordStar 2000's features. The automatic-text-reform feature—normally a delight when editing text—gets in

## WELLINGTON TRAVEL EARNS RECOGNITION

Maria Lentz, Wellington Travel's manager, accepted a plaque in recognition for the outstanding service provided by her company. The presentation was made at the national convention in Chicago last month by Erika Henry, President of the National Association of Travel Consultants.

Wellington Travel has been a member of the Association for the past four years. This is the first national award received--the first of many, says Maria.

Thanks from Maria and her staff to all of our friends who really made this award possible.

## ARGONIA TOUR PACKAGES NOW AVAILABLE

Wellington Travel is now an authorized agent for booking the prestigious Argonia Tours. Argonia schedules tours to exotic locations the world over. These include cruises on the world's most luxurious ocean liners including the Marabelle.

Argonia is also well-known for mountain adventures in the Andes and Himalayas and trips to remote areas like the Australian Outback, Irian Jaya, Indonesia. Also popular are their African safaris. Special interest tours for photographers, artists, musicians, and architects are also available.

Give Wellington Travel a call for further information. These tours are great for awards and bonus incentives.

## ATTENTION FREQUENT TRAVELERS

If you are a frequent traveler for business or pleasure, give one of our agents a call. We are offering some special services to assist you with short-notice reservations when an unexpected trip calls you away.

Remember that we can deliver tickets to your home or office or have them waiting for you when you check in at the airport.

## REPORT FROM HOLLAND
by Sandy Friend

April in Holland is a flower lover's paradise. The international flower show at the Amsterdam Civic Center proved to be a breath-taking fairy land of blooming plants.

I discovered that the Dutch people prefer to leave the plant and its blossoms together. In other words, rather than delivering a bouquet of tulips and daffodils, you'll get the pot, soil, bulbs and all! I can't help but wonder if they'll bloom as well for me next spring.

Art museums and priceless paintings of Rembrandt and others...stained glass windows in massive cathedrals ...pigeons and paupers in the city squares...wooden shoes for tourists...bicycles. These are all familiar sights in Amsterdam.

My favorite? It's hard to choose only one. But I'd have to say it was a dinner-at-dusk boat trip on the canals that thread their way through an array of quaint neighborhoods.

Fig. 13-1/Finished newsletter.

the way when printing multiple columns. This makes it impossible for you to include the centering and the justification commands as you type the text. To center text, you must literally type blank spaces at the beginning of the line to move the heading to a centered position.

Unlike its older sibling WordStar, WordStar 2000 cannot print columns of text justified. Because of the way WordStar 2000 is designed, each line of each column must end with a Return. Lines ending with a Return cannot be justified by WordStar 2000.

To justify text, manually insert blank spaces between words to align them at the right. If you think that unjustified text is easier to read than justified text, you will still be pleased.

The absence of these two features are really not limitations of WordStar 2000. Nearly any word processor with the automatic-text-reform feature would have difficulty maintaining justified and centered text when moving vertical blocks of text.

**If You're Familiar with WordStar**—Several things are different in the way WordStar 2000 and its older sibling work with columns of text. If you have worked with WordStar, you know that you use ^KN to switch to working with column blocks.

With both releases of WordStar, the text is typed on narrowed margins and columns can be displayed side-by-side on the screen, just as they will print. However, with the older WordStar, you can justify the column as you type it, hyphenate words and center headings over the narrow column. When you move text to form multiple columns, the text in all of the columns stay intact. This is because the earlier WordStar does not have an automatic-text-reform feature.

**Typing Text**—To use this method, type the text just as described earlier. However, do not use the centering command to center the headings. If you typed the newsletter following the earlier set of instructions, turn on the display with

^OD

or Shift-F1 and remove the [CENTER] codes with the Backspace or Delete key.

You might find it easier to type the text first, then go back to insert the soft-hyphen commands to have WordStar 2000 hyphenate and print as much as possible on each line.

When hyphens are in place and line breaks are displayed as you want them, go back through the text, pressing Return after each line. This may seem a bit uncomfortable because you are so accustomed to using wordwrap. However, it is necessary to do this to preserve the columns when you mark and move them.

**Changing Soft Hyphens**—The hyphens WordStar 2000 inserted into the text as a result of hyphenation help are displayed brighter on the screen. You need to change each of these soft hyphens into hard hyphens before marking and moving the columns. To do this, move the cursor to the far right side of the line by typing

^CR

or Ctrl-End. Then press the hyphen key which displays a regular hyphen. Turn on the display with

^OD

or Shift-F1 and press the Delete or Backspace key to remove the [HYPHEN] command. You need to do this because the soft hyphen will not print if you simply press Return without typing a required hyphen at the end of the line.

**Marking and Moving the Second Column**—Place the cursor at the left side of the line that will be the first line of the second column. Type

^BV

to turn on the vertical block feature. Then give the Begin Block command

^BB

or F9. Now move the cursor to column 31 or 32 of the last line of the newsletter. Remember that the right margin is set in column 30, and you want to be sure the cursor is past the longest line of text in the column. Give the Block End command by typing

^BE

or by pressing Shift-F9. All of the characters in the last half of the column should be highlighted. If they are not, move the cursor back to the last line of the newsletter, push it further to the right, and give the Block End command again.

**Moving the Column**—Now move the cursor to the first line of the newsletter and set the right margin by typing

^TR

or by pressing Shift-F7 and then typing

70

and pressing Return. Text in the first column should not have moved. If it did, you need to remove the Center command codes or press Return at the end of the lines.

Position the cursor in column 35 of the first line of the newsletter, pressing the Spacebar to move the cursor through the blank space. This is five spaces past the position of the right margin used for typing the column. Give the Block Move command

^BM

or F10. Allow WordStar 2000 just a few seconds and you will see the second column parallel to the first on the screen. Now is the time to insert blank spaces on the heading lines to center them.

You don't want to make changes in the text after the second column has been marked and moved. This may jumble the lines on the screen. If you need to edit text in either of the two columns, again mark the second column as a vertical block and move it below the first column on the screen. Be sure there are enough blank lines below the first column to accommodate the second column when it is moved.

Change the right margin to the setting used when originally typing the text. Then you can edit the columns. To let wordwrap work again, you'll need to remove the Return symbols—the "less than" signs—from the right edge of the screen. When you're done editing and you have again pressed Return to end the text in each line, move the second column alongside the first.

**A Potential Problem**—During printing a peculiar thing may happen. You may see that some of the lines in the second column are indented an additional space beyond the tab setting, or are indented one space from the left margin. This may result when the line in the first column has no text or has only a few words.

Because the text is properly aligned on the screen, you won't see the problem until you print the newsletter. The solution is easy. If the line is indented one space too many, position the cursor at the beginning of the line in the second column and press the Backspace key.

Now on the screen you will see the line "outdented" one space. If the incorrect spacing occurs on the first line of the paragraph, you may need to remove the Tab command and type the two blank spaces. After you compensate on the indented lines by outdenting them, the printing should be done correctly.

## OTHER APPLICATIONS FOR MULTI-COLUMN PRINTING

Once you understand how to type, mark and move columns of text, you can use the commands for formatting the newsletter differently or for creating other kinds of documents. For example, the Wellington Travel newsletter could be printed on the page using the 11-inch edge as the width.

You can also use the vertical block commands to create a question-and-answer format . First, type everything in one column. Then move the answer portion to the second column.

If you are using a dot-matrix or laser printer, you likely also have an array of fonts or typestyles available to you. You can use these to print the headings or the masthead for the newsletter. Remember that when you type ^PF, you see the the typestyles that are available on your dot-matrix printer. If you are using a laser printer, you may need to change cartridges or load the needed fonts into the computer's memory before printing.

This chapter has introduced you to several of the more creative applications of WordStar 2000. Keep in mind that this is simply an introduction. There are other things you can easily do when you use these features of WordStar 2000 and explore the full capabilities of your printer.

# Using MailMerge: 14
# Master Documents
# & Data Files

MailMerge is WordStar 2000's merge-printing feature. Merge printing allows you to quickly produce large quantities of repetitious, yet personalized, documents.

This sounds like a contradiction, but the following example will help explain it: One of the most common uses of MailMerge is to print large quantities of letters. These might be invitations to an open house, a cover letter with a new-product brochure, membership-renewal reminders or a letter of appreciation to your customers. Each letter has the same body. However, each letter is printed with the addressee's inside address and a specific salutation—such as *Dear Jane* rather than *Dear Customer.*

MailMerge makes this possible. It is capable of combining—or *merging*—information from two different files or documents. In this case, one file has the names and addresses of each person receiving the letter. The other file has the body of the letter to be printed for each person in the name-and-address file.

The file with the names and addresses is called the *data file.* You can type it using WordStar 2000 or WordStar 2000's MailList program described in Part III. Often, files produced by popular database programs can also be used for printing with WordStar 2000.

The *master document* is the data file's complementary partner for merge printing. The master document contains the letter or other standard text and codes for retrieving information from the data file.

This chapter shows you how to create the data file and the master document. You will also learn how to print only records that meet certain conditions. There is also information on trouble-shooting if you get some unexpected results during printing.

However, this is just the beginning of WordStar 2000's MailMerge feature. The next chapter will show you how to customize documents even more.

## MAILMERGE DATA FILE

This section explains the most cumbersome way of typing the data file. But don't let that scare you away. This familiarity with the "nuts-and-bolts" requirements of WordStar 2000's merge-data files will help you determine which of your database files or files created with another word processor are compatible with WordStar 2000.

To create a data file, you'll type a long line of information related to each individual on your list. You must do it carefully and accurately—otherwise printing won't be correct. One easier way of creating this file is to use WordStar 2000's MailList.

**Unformatted Format**—You must create the data file using the unformatted format called UNFORM.FRM, one of the formats provided on your WordStar 2000 disks. This creates an unformatted, "generic" document.

When you create a file using UNFORM.FRM, you will notice several differences from the formats you are accustomed to using. Tabs are set every eight columns and there is no right margin. In fact, when editing an unformatted file, you cannot set tabs or margins, or use the indent commands.

Moreover, you also cannot use any of the commands on the Print Enhancements Menu, including boldface, underscore, superscripts and subscripts. Many of the items on the Options Menu are also disabled, including centering, hyphenation, page breaks and justification. In other words, you cannot use any formatting commands when creating an unformatted document.

The information provided by WordStar 2000 at the top of the screen is also different. The cursor's position is specified by line number but never by page number because an unformatted document does not have page breaks.

Before typing the data file, let's look at the way WordStar 2000 requires the data file to be organized. If you have used MailMerge with the older WordStar program, this will look very familiar to you. WordStar and WordStar 2000 use the same data-file format.

**Fields and Records**—All of the information relating to one person in your data file is called a *record*. Each record contains smaller sections or pieces of information called *fields*. For example, let's say that Suzie Swanson is one of the people in your data file. Her record includes fields—last name, first name, title, company name, mailing address, city, state, zip and phone number. This list of fields could go on to include any information you will find useful that relates to Suzie Swanson.

There are two very important things to remember when typing data files. First, WordStar 2000 requires *each* of the records in a data file to have the same number

of fields. In other                    has the nine fields mentioned,
all other records

   Second, the f                            ust be typed in the same order.
When WordStar                          a record, it locates the field by
its position in tl

**Don't Forget C**                          son's record looks like in a
WordStar 200

```
Swanson,S                          el,7454 E.
Broadway                           /947-0808
```

The record                             ill fit on the page. However, on the
computer t                             nding off the right edge of the screen.
If this hap                            ign at the edge of the screen to tell you
that the li

   Notic                              the next field by a comma. Pressing
Return e                              next record. Because each record must
have th                              also understand that each record has the
same n

   Al                                etween the end or beginning of a field and
the se                               ver, include spaces at other places in the
field                                ch as between the words of the company
nam

**Bla**                              xt person on your list. You know the name of
his                                  will you do to make the fields in his record
ma                                   nine fields; Tim's seems to have only eight.

to                                   t still account for it. Although the temptation is
                                     this. It will cause the merge to print incorrectly.
WI                                   commas will be typed together. This indicates
tha                                  as is blank.

```
Tu                          ice Products,1881 Main,Las
Ve                          )2-1972
```

**Comma**                            ping a data file record, a comma signals WordStar
2000 that one field               another begins. However, sometimes a field contains
a comma. For example, Suzie's address may be

```
7454 E. Broadway, Suite 102
```

or Tim's company is

```
Emblem Office Products, Inc.
```

You will use quotation marks to surround fields that contain a comma that must
print. The typed records will look like this:

```
Swanson,Suzie,Manager,E & W Travel,"7454 E. Broadway, Suite
102",Hillsboro,KS,67063,316/947-0808
```

```
Turner,Tim,,"Emblem Office Products, Inc.",1881 Main,Las
Vegas,NV,88903,702/292-1972
```

**Double Quotation Marks**—Let's say that Tim Turner is better known by his nickname Butch. You want his first and last names to print out like this:

```
Tim "Butch" Turner
```

In this example, you want the quotation marks to print. However, if you simply type the quotation marks in the data file, WordStar 2000 understands them to be surrounding a field with commas. The solution is double quotation marks inside quotation marks surrounding the field.

```
Turner,"Tim ""Butch""",,"Emblem Office Products,
Inc.",1881 Main,Las Vegas,NV,88903,702/292-1972
```

**Planning Your Data File**—You can maximize the usefulness of your data file by doing some planning. The information in the data file should meet the needs of your merge-printing projects. In other words, if you will use the data file for printing letters, the fields must contain information that fits the situations you'll encounter in a letter.

For example, to make your typing easy and reduce the number of fields in each record, you might want to combine the first and last name in one field. Before doing this, make a mental inventory of the ways you plan to use the person's name.

How will you address the person in the salutation of a letter? The possibilities vary, depending upon the person's position and your relationship to him or her:

```
Dear Suzie:
```

or

```
Dear Ms..Swanson:
```

or

```
The Honorable Suzie Swanson:
```

If you are on a first-name basis with all of the people on your list, you will want the first and last names in separate fields so you can call out the first name as part of the salutation. However, if you are on a familiar basis with some but not all, you might also want to include a field in the data file that specifies the salutation. Here is Suzie Swanson's record with salutation information in a separate field:

```
Swanson,Suzie,Ms. Swanson,Manager,E & W Travel,"7454 E.
Broadway, Suite 102",Hillsboro,KS,67063,316/947-0808
```

**What to Include in a Data File**—What you choose to include in a data file and the order of the fields within the record is really a matter of personal preference. There is not a right or a wrong way to organize the data file. Of course, a logical order makes it easier to type or read.

## SAMPLE DATA FILE

With this understanding of the data file, let's type records for these people to use for merge printing with the master document you'll type in the next section of this chapter.

Alfonzo Whipple
ALW Enterprises, Inc.
13448 Alpine Overlook
Green Bay, WI 53020
414/448-4800

Ms. Alvena Middleton
1330 Sussex Avenue
Needham, MA 08101
617/927-1313

Dr. Emily Dorson
Armbruster Research Associates, Inc.
212 North Main Street, Suite 2203
Dallas, TX 75012
214/228-1000

Mr. Arvin Ritz
8181 East 18th Circle
Pueblo, CO 86613
303/887-8679

**Planning the Fields** — You will be writing each of these people a letter on behalf of Wellington Travel. The phone number is included in the data file, although it will not be printed in the letter. You might find this useful later for printing a client list. You do not have to use every item in a data file every time you print. Likewise, you can use a selected field more than once in the letter. For example, you might use the first name in the inside address, the salutation and in the body of the letter.

Here is a suggested arrangement for the fields in your data file records:

lastname,firstname,salutation,company,address,city,state,zip,phone.

Remember that records may not have all of these fields. However, using these fields makes it possible to include all of the information required by any of the records.

Create a document named TOURS.DTA. The DTA extension is not required but is helpful to identify this as a data file. Select the UNFORM.FRM format. You are ready to type the entries. Again, you see records here printed on two lines to fit on the page. You will type each record on one long line, pressing Return only to end one record and begin the next. The four records will look like this in the data file:

```
Whipple,Alfonzo,Mr. Whipple,"ALW Enterprises, Inc.",
13448 Alpine Overlook,Green Bay,WI,53020,414/448-4800
Middleton,Ms. Alvena,Alvena,,1330 Sussex Avenue,Needham,
MA,08101,617/927-1313
Dorson,Dr. Emily,Dr. Dorson,"Armbruster Research
Associates, Inc.","212 North Main Street, Suite
2203",Dallas,TX,75012,214/228-1000
Ritz,Mr. Arvin,Mr. Ritz,,8181 East 18th Circle,
Pueblo,CO,86613,303/887-8679
```

When typing is complete, check to see that you have nine fields in each record and that they are in the same order.

## MASTER DOCUMENT

Now it's time for the second step—typing the master document. This is the letter that will go to each of the people in the data file. It has two parts. First is the *command area* that tells MailMerge which data file you want to use. It also lists the order and names the fields in the records. The second part of the master document is the *text area* where you will type the body of the letter.

To type the master document, create a new document named TOURS.MM. The MM extension identifies this as a document that prints with MailMerge. Like the DTA extension, this extension is not required by WordStar 2000 but is added for quick identification. You can use the LETTER.FRM format you created in an earlier chapter or use another format.

**Command Area**—When you type information in the command area at the beginning of the document, you'll use several commands from the MailMerge Menu in Figure 14-1. When you type

^OM

for Option Merge you see this menu on the screen.

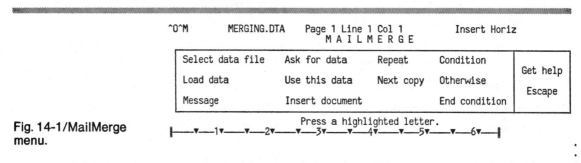

**Fig. 14-1/MailMerge menu.**

**Selecting a Data File**—First, type

^OMS

to Select a data file, or press Alt-8. This tells MailMerge where it needs to go to find the data. The screen prompts

```
Data file to use?
```

and you type

```
TOURS.DTA
```

and press Return. If the data file is on another drive or in another directory on the hard disk, type the drive or directory preceding the filename.

**Naming the Fields**—Once you have told MailMerge which data file to use, you must tell it how to read the file. To let MailMerge identify each of the fields, you give each a name.

These names can be 1 to 31 characters long. They should begin with a letter but can also include numbers and hyphens. To save typing time, keep the names as short as possible while still keeping them meaningful. You can use either capital or lowercase letters. For example, you could type *LASTNAME, lastname* or *LastName.* MailMerge sees them as being the same. Like file names, field names cannot include spaces. Finally, there are three names you should not use for naming a variable—*NOT, AND* and *OR.* MailMerge understands these words as having a special meaning and uses them in another way, as you will see a bit later.

To specify the field names, type

```
^OML
```

for Option MailMerge Load or simply press Alt-9. The prompt

```
Variables to be loaded? (separate with commas)
```

appears on the screen. In response to this question, you will type names for the fields in the data file:

l-name,f-name,salutation,company,address,city,state,zip,phone

The MailMerge information that will be displayed at the top of the screen is

```
[SELECT DATA FILE TOURS.DTA]
[LOAD DATA l-name,f-name,salutation,company,address,city,
state,zip,phone]
```

If you don't see it, turn on the display by typing

```
^OD
```

or Shift-F1.

The names you type here will be typed again later in the text portion of the master document to tell MailMerge where to print each of the fields. You can type up to 64 characters following the Load command. If you need additional space, repeat the Load command and continue typing the variable names.

**Variables**—The field in the data file can also be called a *variable.* The actual information or the *value* of the variable changes in each record, although the name stays the same. For example, each of the records has a first-name variable or field, but the value of the variable is different in each record. The values of the first-name variable in your data file are Alfonzo, Alvena, Emily and Arvin.

**Repeat Command**—There is one more command you need to add at the top of the document to have MailMerge print letters for all of the records in the data file. This is the Repeat Procedure command. Move the cursor back to the Load command line and type

^OMR

for Option MailMerge Repeat, or press Alt-0. When MailMerge asks

Repeat how many times? (Return for end of data)

press Return. This instructs MailMerge to use every record in the data file. If you wanted to print letters only to the first 10 people in the data file, you would type

10

and press Return.

You must type the Repeat command after the Select Data command and before the Load command.

**Text Area**—The next step is to type the text area of the master document. You can start typing the text of the letter immediately below the MailMerge lines at the top of the screen. If you want some blank lines inserted before the first line of the letter prints—probably the date—press Return to move the cursor down.

The role of the text area is two-fold. First, it provides all of the standard parts of the letter. Second, it includes codes that tell MailMerge where to print the values from the data file.

Let's begin typing the letter and you will see how these tasks fall into place. With the cursor positioned below the MailMerge command lines, type the date

May 16, 1986

or the current date and press Return four times to move the cursor to the place in the letter where the inside address begins.

**Ampersands and Variable Names**—To print the inside address, you now need to tell MailMerge to go to the data file, get some information and print it at a specified place. You do this by typing the variable name *exactly* as you typed it at the top of the page after you gave the Load command. (If you don't see the line on the screen now, type ^OD or press Shift-F1 to turn on the display.)

Each of the variable names you type in the text area must be surrounded by ampersands (&). This is the way MailMerge knows you want a value retrieved from the data file rather than having the field name literally printed. You type the variable name where you want the information to print. The first thing you want to retrieve is the addressee's name, which is actually two values. Type

&f-name& &l-name&

pressing the Spacebar between the adjacent ampersands. During printing these codes are replaced by the addressee's name. Press Return to end the line.

Next, you want the company name to print out so you type

&company&

and press Return. Complete the inside address until you have four lines of variable names.

```
&f-name& &l-name&
&company&
&address&
&city&, &state& &zip&
```

Notice the comma typed outside the ampersands between the city and state. It is not part of either of the variable names but will literally print. Note also that there are no spaces between the ampersands and the variable names they surround.

Press Return twice to move the cursor down to where the salutation will print. Type

```
Dear &salutation&:
```

and press Return twice. Now continue typing the body of the letter.

```
Your avid interest in traveling and frequent use of our
services has prompted me to write this letter to you. As
you know, WELLINGTON TRAVEL has a world-wide reputation for
making travel arrangements that are sure to please.

WELLINGTON TRAVEL is now seeking out selected companies and
individuals whose needs for travel accommodations differ a
bit from the average traveler. We're able to book the best
travel schedules, the most convenient and luxurious hotels,
and sight-seeing tours that familiarize you quickly with
your temporary home. Furthermore, we are able to work with
you to organize bonus and incentive trips.

I will be in touch with you shortly, &salutation&, to
discuss our services with you more fully.

Sincerely,

Sidney Russet
Tour Coordinator
WELLINGTON TRAVEL
```

Notice that you used the salutation variable twice in the letter and the phone number was never printed. Remember that you can print the value of a variable any number of times in a document. You also are not required to use every variable in a data record every time you merge print.

**Ending the Page**—At the end of the letter, you tell WordStar 2000 to start printing the next letter on a new page. To do this, position the cursor on a line below the closing and type

```
^OP
```

the Option new Page command. You then see the page break on the screen

```
[PAGE] -------------------------------- -
```

Just below the page break, give MailMerge the Next record command by typing

```
^OMN
```

or pressing Alt-hyphen so it will return to the top of the master document, read another record from the data file and repeat the printing. Be sure that the Next command is typed below the New Page command.

**Merge Print**—Now save the master document using either the Quit and Save command

```
^QS
```

or Alt-1, or the Quit and Print command

```
^QP
```

or Alt-4. The document you will print is TOURS.MM, the master document. Like any other document, the letters will be printed on the printer. While printing, MailMerge reads and carries out the commands at the top of the master document.

**The Problem of Blank Lines**—If you printed the letters now, you'd find that some of the inside addresses had blank lines:

```
Alvena Middleton

1330 Sussex Avenue
Needham, MA 08101
```

and

```
Arvin Ritz

8181 East 18th Circle
Pueblo, CO 86613
```

The blank line appears because the field that was assigned to print on that line was blank in the data file. In this example, neither of the records has a company name.

## CONDITION COMMANDS

To prevent the blank line, you must include a condition command in the master document. To do this, you go back to the master document. Position the cursor at the beginning of the company name line in the inside address. This is the variable MailMerge must evaluate during the printing process. Now you need to tell MailMerge to print the company variable only if it is not blank.

With the cursor at the beginning of the company line, press

```
^OMC
```

for Option MailMerge Condition. MailMerge asks

```
Condition to be evaluated? (maximum 64 characters)
```

You will type

```
company <> " "
```

and press Return.

The statement reads like this: On the condition that the company field is not blank, print the company name. It is important to remember that when you give a condition statement, you must also mark the end of the condition. If you do not end the condition, MailMerge may not print anything beyond the point where the condition statement was given. To do this, move the cursor to the beginning of the address line. Type

```
^OME
```

for Option MailMerge End. Only the company line is included in the condition. When MailMerge encounters the [END CONDITION] command markers, it continues with normal printing.

The inside address in the master document looks like this after giving the condition commands

```
&f-name& &l-name&
[CONDITION company <> ""]
&company&
[END CONDITION]
&address&
&city&, &state& &zip&
```

Notice that in a condition command, you do not surround the variable name—company—with the ampersands as you do in the text portion of the master document.

After the variable name in the condition statement, you type one or two characters that tell MailMerge how to compare or evaluate the condition. The standard equation symbols MailMerge understands are summarized here:

$<>$ means *not equal to*

$=$ means *equal to*

$<$ means *less than*

$<=$ means *less than or equal to*

$>$ means *greater than*

$>=$ means *greater than or equal to*

Finally, on the right-hand side of the condition statement, you tell MailMerge what value the named variable is to be compared with. This value is always enclosed in quotation marks. In the condition statement above, the company variable is compared with a blank—nothing typed between the quotation marks.

If the master document included other potentially blank fields, you would repeat this condition command for each.

**Other Ways to Use the Condition Command**—Let's assume that you have typed many more names into the data file. You now want to be able to select specific records for printing. For example, you may want to select people in a certain state or zip code range. You can specify these simple requirements using MailMerge's condition command. If you are sending a letter to each selected person, you will type the condition command at the top of the text portion of the master document, above the inside address.

To generate letters only to people in Wisconsin, you would give the condition command at the beginning of the text or variable that will print if the condition is true. In this case, put the cursor on the first ampersand of &f-name& in the inside address.

Then type

`^OMC`

and

`state = "WI"`

followed by Return. This defines the terms of the condition. The state must be Wisconsin for the letter to print.

Or perhaps you want to generate letters to those on your list who live in either Wisconsin or Texas. To do this you will use one of MailMerge's logical operators that allow you to have more than one value evaluated. After giving the condition command you would type

`state = "WI" OR state = "TX"`

MailMerge accepts *OR, or* and *Or.* Of course, you could add more states to this condition, up to the 64 characters MailMerge allows.

**Ending the Condition** — This and all other condition commands must have an ending point. The `^OMC` command marks the beginning of the text that prints if the condition is true. The end condition command, `^OME`, marks the end of the text that prints if the condition is true. Because you want the entire letter to print, move the cursor to the end of the letter just above the Next Copy command. Type

`^OME`

and press Return. MailMerge inserts the `[END CONDITION]` code.

**Selecting Ranges** — The previous example let you locate records with the selected field exactly matching a certain condition. You can also have MailMerge locate a specified range for you. You might do this to locate a zip code range or a range of the alphabet.

Let's say that your data file is a membership list for the local chapter of an organization. Someone has volunteered to assist you with calling the members to confirm reservations for an upcoming event. You want a list of everyone whose last name begins with the letters *A* through *K*. In this case your condition statement uses the AND operator

`1-name >= "A" AND 1-name < "L"`

The names selected must be greater than or equal to *A and* less than *L*. You don't use < = K because any letter following *K* in the last name makes the word greater than *K*. This isn't what you want. Notice that MailMerge can determine that letters as well as numbers can be greater than, less than, or equal to another.

You may frequently use this command to select records that fall into a certain zip code range. This is useful to mail to selected portions of a city or region. Again, you will use the AND operator. After giving the condition command, type the beginning and end of the zip code range as you typed the beginning and end of the alphabet range earlier:

```
zip >= "08000" AND zip <= "67217"
```

This tells MailMerge to select all of the zip codes between 08000 and 67217 inclusive.

**Excluding Ranges**—This example can be changed slightly to exclude the records in the zip code range from 08000 to 67217. After giving the condition command, type

```
zip <= "08000" OR zip >= "67217"
```

Two things changed. The "less than" symbols changed to "greater than" symbols and vice versa. Second, the AND changed to OR. This was necessary because no number can be both less than 08000 and greater than 67217.

**Excluding Records With NOT**—The third operator MailMerge understands is NOT. This lets you exclude records that meet certain conditions. They may even fall within a previously selected range. For example, you might want to select all of the records from Texas except those for zip code 75012. You would give the condition command and type

```
State = "TX" AND NOT zip = "75012"
```

This tells MailMerge to select all Texas records but not those with a zip code 75012.

This statement can become even more complex. Perhaps you want to omit another city in Texas. You would type

```
State = "TX" AND NOT (zip = "75012" OR zip = "77511")
```

Notice that parentheses have been added so MailMerge will evaluate the two omitted zip codes together. The statement now says: Select all of the records where the state is Texas except those with the zip codes 75012 or 77511.

The meaning of the statement changes if the parentheses are omitted:

```
State = "TX" AND NOT zip = "75012" OR zip = "77511"
```

It now says: Select all of the records where the state is Texas except those with the zip code 75012, or select records with the zip code 77511. The records with the zip code 77511 will be selected, not omitted as they were in the previous example. This makes the statement redundant because the 77511 city already falls into the Texas selection parameter.

The NOT operator can also be used to omit specific records. Typing

```
NOT state = "TX"
```

in the condition statement omits all of the records where the state value is Texas. You could say the same thing by typing

```
state <> "TX"
```

which says: The state is not equal to Texas. Again, you could omit several states using parentheses. Type

```
NOT (state = "TX" OR state = "WI")
```

meaning that records for both Texas and Wisconsin will be omitted.

**Other Selections and Data-File Design**—What if you want to select records from the data file based on the the area code? For example, to locate all of the records in the area code 214, you can give the condition command and type

```
phone >= "214" and phone < "215"
```

The remaining digits of the phone number following the 214 area code make the number larger than 214. The other part of the requirement is that the number also be less than 215.

Another alternative to this situation is to revise the data file, placing a comma after the area code to put it in a separate field. If you know that you want to be able to recall records based on specific information in the data file, you may find it easiest to to put that information in a field.

## WHAT IF YOU GET SOME PRINTING SURPRISES

If you are new to creating data files, master documents and merge printing, what you hoped you'd get on paper may not be what really happens. It is not a problem with WordStar 2000, nor does it mean that your computer and printer should go to the shop for repairs. The fact is that WordStar 2000 and MailMerge insist on accuracy when you create files. If they cannot find the information you request or cannot carry out the commands you gave, printing may not go smoothly.

The trouble-shooting suggestions here discuss several of the *common* mistakes people make. This is not an all-inclusive list. When some problems are encountered during printing, you will see a message on the screen that should give you a clue about the problem.

There are many combinations of things that can cause unanticipated results. The first reaction is to blame the problems on the computer or WordStar 2000. Although sometimes it seems that these or some other unidentified phantoms are garbling your information, it is usually some little detail you overlooked.

## PROBLEM 1

The variable name rather than the value prints out. When you print your document you see something like *&l-name&* on the printed copy rather than the value from the data file.

**Cause**—Go back to your master document to look for the problem. Check to be sure that the variable name is *exactly* the same in the command area at the top of the file as it is in the text area. For example, if the variable name is 1 - name in the command area, it must be &1-name& in the text area. MailMerge would see a difference between 1-name and 1name. Capitalization should not make a difference. Also keep in mind that the ampersands are used only in the text area of the master document, not in the command area at the top.

## PROBLEM 2

Variables print at the wrong place in the master document. Several seemingly small items in the data file can cause the wrong variables to print so it looks like MailMerge didn't read the variable names in the text area correctly. For example, one printing error may make the beginning of your letter look like this:

```
Emily Dorson
Armbruster Research Associates, Inc.
212 North Main Street
Suite 2203, Dallas TX
```

**Cause**—The problem may be omitted quotation marks. Why are part of the address, the city and state on the same line and why is the zip code omitted? Go back to the data file and you will find that quotation marks do not surround the address field in Emily Dorson's record. It looks like this:

```
Dorson, Emily, Dr. Dorson, "Armbruster Research Associates,
Inc.", 212 North Main Street, Suite
2203, Dallas, TX, 75012, 214/228-1000
```

Remember that MailMerge understands that a comma separates fields. Each time it comes to a comma, it assumes that a new field has started. Therefore, MailMerge read 212 North Main Street as the address, Suite 2203 as the city, Dallas as the state and TX as the zip code.

Actually, the record with the omitted quotation mark is not as severely affected as the one following it. Arvin Ritz's record is the next one in the data file. The inside address on his letter is more confused:

```
Ritz 214/228-1000
Arvin
8181 East 18th Circle, Pueblo CO
```

When Emily Dorson's record is corrected, Arvin Ritz's letter will also print correctly.

**Cause**—It may be unpaired quotation marks. In addition to completely omitting a pair of quotation marks, you might forget only one. This also produces undesired results. Let's look at Emily Dorson's record with the quotation mark after the company name omitted.

```
Dorson, Emily, Dr. Dorson, "Armbruster Research Associates,
Inc., "212 North Main Street, Suite
2203", Dallas, TX, 75012, 214/228-1000
```

The omission of the closing quotation mark on the company field will print the inside address like this:

```
Dr. Emily Dorson
Armbruster Research Associates, Inc.,212 North Main Street
Suite 2203"
Dallas, TX 75012
```

When the quotation mark is missing, only the current record misprints. The following record prints correctly.

**Cause**—Suppose blank fields are unaccounted for. Several of the records you typed in the data file have blank fields. For example, Alvena Middleton does not have a company name—that value is blank. When a field is blank, you must still account for it by typing the comma that ends the field. Done correctly, the record looks like this

```
Middleton,Alvena,Alvena,,1330 Sussex
Avenue,Needham,MA,08101,617/927-1313
```

If this seemingly insignificant piece of punctuation is omitted, MailMerge will not print correctly. The result may be something like this

```
Alvena Middleton
1330 Sussex Avenue
Needham
MA, 08101 617/927-1313
```

Why? Remember the MailMerge Load command you used at the top of the master document? This told MailMerge the order of the variables in the record. When the comma is omitted, each value is read before its turn, so it will print at the wrong place in the merged document. The rest of the records in the data file are also printed incorrectly. However, adding the missing comma also corrects the records that follow.

**Cause**—You will get another surprise during printing if the data items are typed in the wrong order. In our sample data file, the last-name variable was typed before the first name. If these were typed in reverse order like this

```
Alvena,Middleton,,Alvena,,1330 Sussex
Avenue,Needham,MA,08101,617/927-1313
```

MailMerge would not print the address correctly using the other information you have given it in the master document. The address will look like this, assuming that the MailMerge Load command is the same as shown earlier in this chapter:

```
Middleton Alvena
1330 Sussex Avenue
Needham, MA 08101
```

**Cause**—Another common problem results from having too few fields in a record. For example, let's say that the data file records have only the name and address information. The telephone number we included earlier is not included in the new data file. Then let's say that the comma marking an empty field in Alvena Middleton's record is omitted.

```
Middleton,Alvena,Alvena,1330 Sussex
Avenue,Needham,MA,08101
```

Two errors result. First, the values will print in the wrong place, as happened in one of the examples earlier. Second, because Alvena's record does not have the number of variables listed in the Load command in the master document, MailMerge "borrows" the first variable from the next record. The result may print as follows:

```
Alvena Middleton
1330 Sussex Avenue
Needham
MA, 08101 Dorson
```

Again, all of the following records print incorrectly.

## PROBLEM 3

Incorrect spacing between words. When the letters print, you may find that too many or too few spaces were included between words. If the merged documents print with too many spaces between words, look at two places.

**Cause**—Extra spaces may be in the data line. First, check the data file. Remember that you don't want to type spaces before or after commas that separate fields. An incorrectly typed record might look like this

```
Ritz, Arvin, Mr. Ritz, , 8181 East 18th Circle, Pueblo, CO,
86613,303/887-8679
```

The extra spaces in the data file cause extra spaces to print during the merge.

**Cause**—The second place to look for the cause of extra blank spaces is in the master document where you typed the variable names surrounded by ampersands. If your data file is typed correctly without extra blank spaces, you control the spacing between words in the master document. For example, because you want a space between the addressee's first and last names, you type the variable names like this:

```
&f-name& &l-name&
```

with one space between the ampersands in the middle of the line. If the values run together in the printed document, `AlvenaMiddleton`, you forgot the space between the variable names.

```
&f-name&&l-name&
```

## PROBLEM 4

Conditions don't work properly. Condition commands in MailMerge are very helpful in selecting the desired records from the data file. However, MailMerge requires accuracy in the commands. If the condition commands are not being executed as you anticipated, there are several items you should check.

**Cause**—You may have omitted a condition command. Remember that when you give a condition command

```
^OMC
```

you must also mark the place where the condition ends by typing

```
^OME
```

If the end condition command is omitted, you may be inadvertently asking MailMerge to evaluate too many conditions, and no records are found that meet the condition. Printing may stop.

**Cause**—The trouble may be variable-name discrepancy. When you type a variable name in the condition, you must be certain that the name exactly matches the way you typed it in the command area of the master document. For example, if the Load command includes l - name and f - name as names for two of the fields, MailMerge will not make the connection if you type lname and fname, or something else as inexact.

Also, do not include a space between the variable name and the ampersand. This causes the variable name rather than the value to print. For example, if the variable name is city and you type

```
& city&
```

MailMerge will literally print & c i t y& rather than the value.

**Cause**—There may be ampersands in the condition statement. When you want the value of a variable to print, you enclose it in ampersands. For example, at the place in the merged document where the city is to print, you type

```
&city&
```

However, when you give a condition command, you do not enclose the variable name in ampersands. Earlier in this chapter, you used the condition command to check the company field and print something on the line only if the company field was not blank. After giving the condition command

```
^OMC
```

you typed

```
company <> " "
```

without ampersands to mean that the company name would be printed in the inside address if it was not blank.

## SUMMARY

You now have a good understanding of the way WordStar 2000's MailMerge feature works. Continue to the next chapter to discover more ways you can make this powerful program perform for you.

# *Using MailMerge:* 15
# *Advanced Features*

The previous chapter introduced you to the basics of using MailMerge. Once the data file and master document are in place, you can use more of MailMerge's powerful commands to tailor documents to your needs.

For example, if you are in business, you might want to send a letter to all of your customers. However, the letters going to customers in Oklahoma may need an extra paragraph. Or, the Oklahoma letters need a paragraph substituted in the place of one that goes to customers in other states. To do this you will combine the Condition command you used in the previous chapter with the Otherwise command.

You use the Ask For Data command to type information from the keyboard during merge printing. This lets you insert information into the merge printed document that isn't included in the data file. To help you know what information you need to type, you can have MailMerge display a message on the screen. For example, MailMerge may be set to ask you for the name of the product the addressee has recently purchased. However, you will find it difficult to type the name of the product if you don't know which customer MailMerge is referring to. The Message command can then be used to display the customer's name.

You can also set the value of a certain variable in the master document. For example, the master document may include the variable name &date& to print the date at the top of the letter. However, the data file does not have a field named date. The Use Data For Variable command is one of the ways you can set the date that will print on each letter. You will give the command at the top of the master document and type the date you want MailMerge to use.

MailMerge can also print a series of files with the Insert command. You tell MailMerge the order in which you want documents to be inserted during printing. You might use this, for example, to construct a document by printing any number of other documents. This could be used to write letters by joining several paragraph files or to print several chapters of a book as one document without giving the print command between chapters.

## USING THE OTHERWISE COMMAND

In the previous chapter you typed a letter named TOURS.MM on behalf of Wellington Travel that went to each person in the data file. Now let's assume that you want this letter to go to everyone on the list *except* those who live in Wisconsin or Texas. The letter going to clients in Wisconsin and Texas will substitute a paragraph for the last one used in the other letters.

First, you will give the Condition command you used in the previous chapter. Position the cursor at the beginning of the last paragraph, type

```
^OMC
```

and

```
state = "TX" OR state = "WI"
```

pressing Return to end the statement.

When the screen display is on you see

```
[CONDITION state = "TX" OR state = "WI"]
```

Next, you type the paragraph that will be included in the letter when the condition is true.

```
I will be in &city& within the next few weeks and will call
to set up an appointment to discuss our services.
```

The command now says that this paragraph will be printed if the state is Wisconsin or Texas. The next thing you must do is tell MailMerge what to print if the state is not Wisconsin or Texas. This is where you use the Otherwise command.

Position the cursor below the new paragraph you typed that goes to Wisconsin and Texas clients. Now give the Otherwise command by typing

```
^OMO
```

for Option MailMerge Otherwise. The paragraph that originally was the last paragraph of the letter will go to everyone not in Texas or Wisconsin.

To finish the command sequence, you must mark the location of the end of the condition. Place the cursor after the "Otherwise" paragraph and type

```
^OME
```

When the display is on, this portion of the document looks like this on the screen:

```
[CONDITION state = "TX" OR state = "WI"]
I will be in &city& within the next few weeks and will call
to set up an appointment to discuss our services.
```

```
[OTHERWISE]
```
I will be in touch with you shortly, &salutation&, to discuss our services with you more fully.
```
[END CONDITION]
```

## USING THE ASK FOR DATA COMMAND

Sometimes you want to be able to include information in a merge printed document that is not included in the data file. Let's say, for example, that you and Sidney Russet are each writing some of the letters for Wellington Travel. The letters are exactly the same except for the name in the closing. You want your name on the letters going to your clients. Sidney's name will go on the others.

Rather than typing your name or Sidney's name repeated in the data file, you can give MailMerge the correct name during the printing. You will tell MailMerge to ask for the value of a variable. You will also mark the place in the master document where this variable will print.

**Having MailMerge Ask** — Adding the Ask For Data command to the master document is easy. Go back to to the document named TOURS.MM. Position the cursor below the last command line at the top of the screen. Type

`^OMA`

for Option Merge Ask. MailMerge prompts

`Variable name to ask for? ......`

You want MailMerge to ask you for the name of the person who will sign the letter in the closing so type

`signature`

and press Return. Notice that this variable is not surrounded by commas, quotation marks or ampersands. Next, MailMerge asks

`Question to display when asking?`

You can type up to 54 characters that will be displayed on the screen to prompt the user. Type

`Who will sign this letter?`

and press Return. MailMerge then asks

`Maximum characters in response? 10`

Unless you type another number, 10 will be used. Change the number by typing

`40`

which is the largest number you can use. This will allow you plenty of room to type your name or Sidney Russet's. Press Return.

MailMerge has now embedded another code in the master document. When the display is turned on you see

```
[ASK FOR signature WITH PROMPT "Who will sign this letter?"
MAXIMUM LENGTH 40]
```

**Marking the Position for Printing**—The first part of the Ask For Data command is done—getting MailMerge to ask the question. Next, you must tell MailMerge where to print the information you give it. Move the cursor to the closing of the letter. Remove Sidney Russet's name. Type

```
&signature&
```

in its place. This is where you want the value to print. The closing of the letter in the master document now reads like this

```
Sincerely,

&signature&
Tour Coordinator
WELLINGTON TRAVEL
```

## USING THE MESSAGE COMMAND

When MailMerge asks you to type a signature, you may not always know which client MailMerge is referring to. So you can request MailMerge to display a message telling you the name. Position the cursor on the Ask For Data command you typed earlier in the master document. Type

```
^OMM
```

to give the Option MailMerge Message command. MailMerge prompts

```
Message to be displayed? (maximum 79 characters)
```

so you can specify the message you want to see. Type

```
This letter goes to &f-name& &l-name&
```

and press Return. This is the completed command line when the display is turned on.

```
[MESSAGE This letter goes to &f-name& &l-name&]
```

During the merge print, the variable names are substituted with values. For example, you will see

```
This letter goes to Alvena Middleton
```

on the screen while this letter prints.

The command area at the top of the master document now looks like this

```
[SELECT DATE FILE TOURS.MM]
[REPEAT UNTIL END OF DATA]
[LOAD DATA l-name,f-name,salutation,company,address,city,
state,zip,phone]
[MESSAGE This letter goes to &f-name& &l-name&]
[ASK FOR signature WITH PROMPT "Who will sign this letter?"
MAXIMUM LENGTH 40]
```

## USING THE USE DATA FOR VARIABLE COMMAND

Now let's assume that you have accepted responsibility for Sidney Russet's clients in this data file. You want to tell MailMerge that when it encounters &signature& in the master document, you always want your name to print. If you are trying this example, remove the Ask For Data command that is currently at the top of the master document. Another command takes its place.

Type

^OMU

for Option MailMerge Use so MailMerge will use the data you provide for each occurrence of the variable name. You see the prompt

Field name for data value?

and you type

signature

and press Return. You want to provide the data for the signature variable. Then MailMerge asks

Data value to use?

and you type your name and press Return. The data you type here can be up to 52 characters long. MailMerge inserts a code

[USE (Your Name) FOR signature]

so each time you print this master document, your name will automatically be supplied for the signature.

**Using System Variables**—There are five variables that the MailMerge system is capable of supplying without the use of the data file or the Use Data command. These are the date, the page number, the line number, the time, and the filename.

**Date Variable**—Let's say, for example, that you want MailMerge to supply the date at the top of the master document. Because you use the letter frequently, you can save time by not going to the master document each time to change the date.

To do this, remove the date from the master document. In its place type

&%date&

The percent sign identifies this as a system variable. The computer provides the information; you do not. The variable name is enclosed in ampersands to identify it as a variable. Without the ampersands, *%date* would print literally. The current date would not be substituted.

Where does MailMerge get the date? When you load the WordStar 2000 program, the disk operating system asks for the date. That is the date the operating system uses for marking the creation date for files on the disk. It retains this information until the computer is turned off. Some computers have a built-in clock on one of the cards inside. The clock automatically records the current date and time without asking you for them when you turn on the computer. WordStar 2000 types the date in this format: May 16, 1986.

**Other Variables**—Here are the other variables the computer can provide in a document:

**&%page&**—This is the current page number. You have already used this one to mark the position of the page number in any printed document.

**&%line&**—The current line number.

**&%time&**—The current time in the hour:minute:second format. For example, 10:15:00 means 10:15 a. m.

**&%filename&**—The name of the document being printed.

## USING THE INSERT DOCUMENT COMMAND

The MailMerge Insert command lets you insert entire documents one inside another. For example, the master document may contain a series of insert commands to chain or link files together during printing. To do this, type the Insert command

```
^OMI
```

which prompts MailMerge to ask

```
Document to be inserted?
```

Type the name of the document to be inserted at this point including the drive or directory identifier if necessary. To chain print several chapters of a book, the master document might have only insert commands in it. To begin each chapter on a new page, include the new page command between the insert commands. There is no limit to the number of files you can chain print using the Insert command. The commands will look like this on the screen with the display turned on

```
[INSERT DOCUMENT B:CHAP1]
[PAGE]-------------------------------
[INSERT DOCUMENT C:\WS2\CHAP2]
[PAGE]-------------------------------
[INSERT DOCUMENT B:CHAP3]
[PAGE]-------------------------------
[INSERT DOCUMENT C:\WS2\CHAP4]
```

Chapters 2 and 4 are on Drive C, in directory WS2.

The master document can contain text along with the insert command already in the master document. For example, you may want to insert a table from another file into the report you are typing. Position the cursor at the point where the table is to print and give the insert command

```
^OMI
```

followed by the name of the document when MailMerge asks. During printing, Mail Merge will retrieve and print the requested file at the point of the command.

## USING MAILMERGE TO PRINT LABELS

So far, I have assumed that you want to print letters using the names and addresses in the data file. However, what do you do if you want the information in a data file printed on mailing labels or envelopes? First, you need to know the size of the label you are working with. How high and how wide is it? Let's assume that we are working with a standard label 3-1/2 inches wide and 15/16 inch high.

**1-Across Label Format**—If you are printing labels, you need to use a format that will print the information correctly on a label this size. Press

F

at the Opening Menu to begin the format design. Name the format

`1ACROSS.FRM`

and press Return. Accept the default font for your printer and single spacing, 6.00 LPI. Set the size of the top and bottom margins to zero. Change the number of lines per page to 6. The distance from the top of one label to the top of the next is one inch, so the label, or "page," is 6 lines. Also change the odd and even page offset to zero. Specify that the text be printed ragged-right rather than justified, and type N for No to both automatic hyphenation and use of form feeds. Save this format.

**1-Across Label Master Document**—Now create a master document that will print the desired information on the 1-across labels. Name the document

`1ACROSS.MM`

to identify it as the MailMerge file for printing 1-across labels. Use the 1ACROSS.FRM format.

This master document is created like the ones you use for other merge printing. The master document will look like this:

```
[SELECT DATA FILE TOURS.DTA]
[REPEAT UNTIL END OF DATA]
[LOAD DATA f-name,l-name,salutation,company,address,city,
state,zip,phone]
&f-name& &l-name&
[CONDITION company <> ""]
&company&
[END CONDITION]
&address&
&city&, &state& &zip&
[PAGE]----------------------------
[NEXT COPY]
```

**3-Across Label Format**—Let's assume that the 3-across labels also measure 15/16 inch high by 3-1/2 inches wide. Name the format for printing these labels

`3ACROSS.FRM`

and press Return. Select the default font for your printer and single spacing, 6.00 LPI. Set the top and bottom margins to zero as you did for the 1ACROSS.FRM format file.

Now let's look at the right margin. Each of the three labels across the page is 3-1/2 inches wide. Assuming 10 characters per inch, each of the labels can print 35 characters for a total of 105 characters across the page of labels. So set the right margin to 105.

Next you'll set a tab to mark the beginning of each label. The first label uses spaces 1 through 35 so the second label begins with space 36. Set a tab every 36 spaces. Answer the remaining questions on the format menu as you did in the 1ACROSS.FRM format. Save this format.

**3-Across Label Master Document**—You now tell MailMerge where to print the desired information. You are actually printing three labels across each "page." To print across the line, MailMerge must load three sets of variables.

Name this master document 3ACROSS.MM. You will type the command area just like that of the 1ACROSS.MM master document except you will define three sets of variable names, one for each of the labels across the page.

The command area of this master document will look like this:

```
[SELECT DATA FILE TOURS.DTA]
[REPEAT UNTIL END OF DATA]
[LOAD DATA l-name1,f-name1,salutation1,company1,address1,
city1,state1,zip1]
[LOAD DATA phone1]
[LOAD DATA l-name2,f-name2,salutation2,company2,address2,
city2,state2,zip2]
[LOAD DATA phone2]
[LOAD DATA l-name3,f-name3,salutation3,company3,address3,
city3,state3,zip3]
[LOAD DATA phone3]
```

Now you're ready to type the text area to show MailMerge exactly where to print each of the values so they will fit properly on the labels. At the left margin, type

```
&f-name1& &l-name1&
```

to have the values for the first record printed on the first label. Next you want the values for the second record to be printed on the same line but on the next label. To accomplish this, you type

```
^PN
```

the No New Line command. The cursor moves to the next line on the screen and a hyphen appears at the far right edge of the screen. This is WordStar 2000's symbol to mark that a new line will not start during printing. This is one time when what you see on the screen differs from what will be printed.

The second record prints beginning at the tab in column 36. Press the Tab key, then type

```
&f-name2& &l-name2&
```

followed by another

```
^PN
```

so printing will continue on the same line. And finally, you type the variable names for the third record. Press the Tab key twice to move the cursor to the position of the third label, type

```
&f-name3& &l-name3&
```

and press Return. You use Return this time because you want a new line to begin. Repeat these steps for each of the values.

You will see the variable names displayed in staggered positions on the screen.

```
&f-name1& &l-name1&
          &f-name2& &l-name2&
                    &f-name3& &l-name3&
&company&
          &company&
                    &company&
```

Remember that because you used the ^PN command, these staggered lines will actually print on the same line. You will notice also that the line number at the top of the page doesn't change when the cursor moves across these lines.

Again, when all of the variable names have been typed in position, type the new page command

```
^OP
```

and press Return followed by

```
^OMN
```

to have MailMerge read the next set of records.

You could also type this master document like this:

```
&f-name1& &l-name1&      &f-name2& &l-name2&      &f-name3& &l-name3&
&company1&               &company2&               &company3&
&address1&               &address2&               &address3&
&city1&, &state1& &zip1&  &city2&, &state2& &zip2&  &city3&, &state3& &zip3&
```

The master document typed here will not omit the blank lines on the label that result from a blank field. Doing this creates a vastly more complex master document. A much easier way is to use the LABEL3.LST file that is available with the MailList program.

**Envelope Format**—In addition to printing mailing labels, you can print names and addresses directly on the envelope. For example, after printing letters to a group of people from a data file, you can print envelopes in the same order for each person. A revision of the format you used for printing labels will serve you well. In fact, you can copy the entire 1ACROSS.MM document for use with envelopes.

To copy the document, type

```
C
```

for Copy at the Opening Menu. When WordStar 2000 asks

`File to copy from?`

you type

`1ACROSS.MM`

or move the highlight bar to it and press Return. Then WordStar 2000 wants to know

`File to copy to?`

so you type

`ENVELOPE.MM`

and press Return.

Now you need to make a change in the format of the document so type

`F`

at the Opening Menu. When WordStar 2000 asks

`Format or formatted document name?`

type

`ENVELOPE.MM`

and press Return. This time you won't be able to move the highlight bar and press Return. Notice that WordStar 2000 shows you only the names of the format files, not document files.

Press Return to accept the current answers in this format until you reach the page offset questions. Change both the odd and even page offsets from 10 to 40. This means that the lines of the address will begin printing 40 spaces from the left edge of the envelope, an appropriate placement on business size envelopes. Printing will begin at the printhead when you use the ENVELOPE.MM document. The top margin is zero, so WordStar 2000 will not move down additional lines before printing the first line.

There are two things to keep in mind when printing envelopes. First, make sure that the same filename follows the MailMerge Select command in the ENVELOPE.MM file and the master document of the letter you printed. If this isn't the case, you will have many letters and many envelopes, but they won't match!

Second, when you give the Print command, you need to ask WordStar 2000 to pause printing between pages so you can roll another envelope into the printer. If you're accustomed to using continuous feed paper, this can be an easy item to overlook.

This completes Part II of this book, an overview of the things you can do with WordStar 2000 and MailMerge. Part III continues with a description of the features in WordStar 2000 Plus.

# Part III
# Using WordStar
# 2000 Plus.

Welcome to Part III. Its three chapters cover the main features of the WordStar 2000 Plus program. Basically this is WordStar 2000 with all of the "bells and whistles." WordStar 2000 Plus incorporates all of the features of WordStar 2000 already discussed plus a mail-list program, an indexing program and a telecommunications package. These useful features make WordStar 2000 even more versatile and exciting.

**MailList** is a program the provides a fill-in screen for typing the information you usually include for mailing labels and envelopes. The names, addresses, phone numbers and much more are typed easily and quickly. These data files are very useful for printing with MailMerge.

**StarIndex** reads special commands typed in a document and creates tables of contents, indexes and numbers headings in a document. You will find this useful when working with longer documents like reports and books.

**TelMerge** is a communications program. With it, your computer can "converse" with another via phone lines. It includes information for calling most of the popular electronic mail and computer-information services.

# 16 Using MailList To Prepare Data Files

MailList works hand-in-hand with MailMerge, discussed in chapters 14 and 15. MailList is designed to provide a fill-in screen for creating the data files that you use with MailMerge. This eliminates the need for you to type the data files, carefully counting the commas and fields to be sure everything is perfect. Essentially, MailList is the easier, short-cut method.

## MAILLIST FEATURES

If you're familiar with DataStar, a companion to WordStar, you'll recognize some similarities to MailList. Unlike DataStar, however, MailList is in a fixed, programmed form. Information frequently required in preparation of a mailing list is included.

Once you type information into the MailList file, the information can be sorted on one of the fields as you wish. You can also define parameters for viewing records. For example, you can ask MailList to show you only the records for people living in Texas. Note that this feature is for viewing records only. It doesn't affect the records that will print. Printing is still controlled with the condition commands in the MailMerge document.

You can create any number of MailList data files just like you can have many MailMerge data files. If you are using a hard disk, you can type up to 65,535 records in one file—enough to amply cover most everyone's needs. However, if you want to be able to sort the records, you'll need to keep the number of records down to about 30,000. The sorting you do with MailList literally rearranges the order of the records in the file.

MailList also provides several MailMerge print-command files. These are convenient for printing labels, envelopes, phone lists and a proof list that prints all of the information for each record in the data file.

Although you now know that MailList is closely related to the tasks of MailMerge, you may wonder what it can do for you specifically? Or, why is it included in the WordStar 2000 Plus package? The answer is that it makes several tasks easier for you, as follows:

**Data File Creation**—MailList's primary task is to let you create data files less tediously than typing long lines of words and commas as you did in the previous two chapters. MailList provides a clear fill-in screen as shown in Figure 16-1. As you type information, MailList adds the commas, quotation marks and Returns. Although you cannot change this screen, it includes the most frequently used fields for the average data file. Notice too that it gives you three user fields and three remark fields that you can use for typing information of your choice.

```
         A D D   N E W   R E C O R D S          A:WS2LIST.DTA
 ┌──────────────────────────────────────────────────┬──────────┐
 │ ^Copy from previous record  ^Write/save record in file │ ^Get help │
 │                                                    │ Escape   │
 └──────────────────────────────────────────────────┴──────────┘
              Type data and press Return.

   Record Number: 00000

First, Initial, Last: _____ __ _____    Mr./Ms.: _____
              Title: _____

           Company: _____
     Address Line 1: _____
     Address Line 2: _____
    City, State, Zip: _____ __ _____
           Country: _____
             Phone: _____  Date 00/00/00   type date as mm/dd/yy

      User Fields-           Remarks-
              1: _____   _____
              2: _____   _____
              3: _____   _____
```

Fig. 16-1/MailList's fill-in screen.

**Selecting Specific Records**—Once you have typed information in a data file, you can have MailList display records on the screen that meet certain specifications. MailList calls the selection criterion a *filter*. For example, you might want to see all of the records for people living in Dallas or all of those with the last name Johnson. With the View option you can page through all of the records that meet the requirement. However, if you printed the data file, all of the records would print unless condition commands were included in the MailMerge document. The View command has no influence on the selection of specific records for merge printing.

**Sorting**—All of the records in a data file can be sorted on some specific information. For example, if you are doing a mailing, you'll likely want the records in zip code order. This will let you print letters, envelopes, and mailing labels in the same zip code order. You can also sort the records to put them in alphabetical order based on the last name, the company name or the state. You can sort the same data file any number of times based on different criteria.

**Editing**—Once you have typed a data file, you can use MailList to easily make changes in it. You can page through the data file in the order the records were typed or the order in which they are currently sorted. You can also move through the records based on the current filter, making changes to a record when it is displayed.

**Printing**—You can print any information from the MailList data file using MailMerge commands. The printing can be done to the printer or to a disk file. You can insert information from the data file into letters and other documents or print them as mailing labels, envelopes or reports. The MailList data file may contain more information than you will ever include in a single printed document.

As with the MailMerge documents created in the previous two chapters, you may choose to include only selected variable values during printing. You can use the same variable more than once in the same document.

Generally, it is not the task of a word processor to store, manipulate and sort information. More commonly, a *data base* program does this. If you have large amounts of data to keep track of, a data base program will do a much better job than MailList. Although the power and flexibility of MailList does not compare with popular data base programs, it is a convenient feature to have closely linked with WordStar 2000. It is designed to quickly and easily manage information you use in creating mailing lists for use with MailMerge.

## CREATING A MAILLIST DATA FILE

Let's go through the steps for creating a data file using MailList. You can see the MailList option on the second screen of the Opening Menu by pressing the Spacebar as prompted. You access the MailList program by typing

L

at the Opening Menu. It isn't necessary to see the MailList option on the screen to have WordStar 2000 load the program for you.

If you are using a computer with two floppy disk drives, WordStar 2000 will inform you that it can't find WS2LIST.COM. It needs to have this program on the disk in Drive A. When the message appears, remove the WordStar 2000 disk from Drive A and replace it with a *copy* of the Advanced Features disk. (Remember that you should not use the original disks that came with WordStar 2000 Plus.) Then press Return.

When using a hard disk, WordStar 2000 looks in the current directory for WS2LIST.DTA. If you are not in the current directory, you will see a message saying that WS2LIST.DTA can't be found. Solve this by typing

D

at the Opening Menu, then typing

\WS2000

to change the directory.

Later, when you are done using MailList, WordStar 2000 will tell you that it cannot find the WS2000.EXE program on the disk. This is the time to remove the Advanced Features from Drive A and reinsert the WordStar 2000 program disk.

If you are using MailList on a computer with a hard disk, the computer will look for the MailList programs in the directory with the other WordStar 2000 program files and the computer will load the program as commanded.

When MailList is loaded, you see the menu shown in Figure 16-2.

```
          M A I L L I S T   M E N U          A:WS2LIST.DTA

 ┌──────────────────────────────────────────────┬────────────┐
 │  Choose a data file    Locate records by number │  Get help  │
 │                                                │            │
 │  Add new records       Sort records            │  Quit      │
 │                                                │            │
 │  View and edit records                         │            │
 └──────────────────────────────────────────────┴────────────┘

              Press a highlighted letter.
```

Fig. 16-2/MailList menu.

**Choosing a Data File**—Before you start typing records onto the MailList screen, you need to tell MailList where you want the records stored. To do this, type

C

for Choose a data file. MailList then asks

Data file or directory to use?

so you type a disk drive letter if necessary or a directory name followed by

TOUR-LST.DTA

and press Return. When naming a MailList data file, the only extension you should use is .DTA. If you do not select the Choose option from the menu, MailList automatically puts the records in a file named *WS2LIST.DTA*.

**Adding New Records**—When you have specified the storage file, MailList returns you to the menu. This time type

A

to Add new records. The MailList screen shown earlier in Figure 16-1 is displayed.

When you begin work on a new data file, MailList gives you the opportunity to type the record number at the top of the screen. Numbering will begin with 00001 unless you type another starting number. If you type another number, MailList will sequentially number each record from the specified starting number. Be certain that all of the records you will type will fit between your starting number and 99999. In other words, if you give a starting number of 99989, you will be able to type only 10 records in that data file. MailList gives you an opportunity to type a record number only on the first record of the data file.

Once you decide on a starting number, MailList automatically numbers the rest of the records sequentially.

**Moving the Cursor**—To move the cursor within one of the fields, you use some of the familiar WordStar 2000 commands, as shown in the accompanying table, Figure 16-3.

## CURSOR MOVEMENT WITHIN FIELDS

| To Move | You Type |
|---|---|
| Character left | Left-arrow or ^S |
| Character right | Right-arrow or ^D |
| Next field | Return or ^F or Ctrl-Right arrow |
| Previous field | Shift-Tab or ^A |
| Top of screen | Home or ^T |
| Bottom of screen | End or ^L |
| Delete character left | Backspace |
| Delete character at cursor | Delete |

Fig. 16-3

**Copying Fields**—When you type records, you might notice that the information for one or more fields stays the same from record to record. For example, you may have several successive records with the same company name, city, state or zip code. To save typing time, you can have MailList fill in the information that appeared in the same field of the previous file.

With the cursor in the repetitious field, type

^C

to Copy from the previous record. MailList immediately fills in the information for you.

**Saving the Record** — When typing is complete, type

`^W`

to Write the record to the disk file. MailList then gives you three more choices.

`Save the data by pressing Return.`

Pressing Return saves the records and displays a blank screen with the next sequential number.

`Return to the form and Continue with Spacebar.`

If you discovered you needed to make more changes, press the Spacebar. MailList returns the record to the screen.

`Return to the MailList menu with Esc.`

Pressing the Escape key redisplays the MailList Menu. The most recent record is not saved.

   To compare the preparation of data files with MailList and the method described in Chapter 14, let's type the names of four people used in the MailMerge examples. Here again are their names, addresses, and phone numbers, shown as they should appear on the screen. Press Return after typing each field to move the cursor to the next one.

```
              A D D   N E W   R E C O R D S        B:WS2LIST.DTA
 ┌─────────────────────────────────────────────────────────┬──────────┐
 │ ^Copy from previous record    ^Write/save record in file │ ^Get help│
 │                                                          │          │
 │                                                          │ Escape   │
 └─────────────────────────────────────────────────────────┴──────────┘
               Type data and press Return.


      Record Number: 00001  Alfonzo Whipple

First, Initial, Last: Alfonzo___ __ Whipple_____     Mr./Ms.: Mr._____
              Title: _____

           Company: ALW Enterprises, Inc._____
    Address Line 1: 13448 Alpine Overlook_____
    Address Line 2: _____
  City, State, Zip: Green Bay_____ WI 53020_____
           Country:
             Phone: 414/448-4800____ Date 00/00/00    type date as mm/dd/yy

       User Fields-                  Remarks-
               1: _____          _____
               2: _____          _____
               3: _____          _____
```

Fig. 16-4/MailList screen.

```
               A D D   N E W   R E C O R D S          B:WS2LIST.DTA
     ┌──────────────────────────────────────────────┬──────────────┐
     │ ^Copy from previous record    ^Write/save record in file │ ^Get help │
     │                                                │              │
     │                                                │ Escape       │
     └──────────────────────────────────────────────┴──────────────┘
                        Type data and press Return.


           Record Number: 00002  Alvena Middleton

     First, Initial, Last: Alvena_____ ___ Middleton____    Mr./Ms.: Ms._____
                    Title: _____

                  Company: _____
           Address Line 1: 1330 Sussex Avenue_____
           Address Line 2: _____
        City, State, Zip: Needham_____  MA 08101_____
                  Country:
                    Phone: 617/927-1313____ Date 00/00/00   type date as mm/dd/yy

              User Fields-              Remarks-
                    1: _____       _____
                    2: _____       _____
                    3: _____       _____
```

Fig. 16-5/MailList
screen.

```
               A D D   N E W   R E C O R D S          B:WS2LIST.DTA
     ┌──────────────────────────────────────────────┬──────────────┐
     │ ^Copy from previous record    ^Write/save record in file │ ^Get help │
     │                                                │              │
     │                                                │ Escape       │
     └──────────────────────────────────────────────┴──────────────┘
                        Type data and press Return.


           Record Number: 00003  Emily Dorson

     First, Initial, Last: Emily_____ ___ Dorson_____    Mr./Ms.: Dr._____
                    Title: _____

                  Company: Armbruster Resrch. Assoc., Inc
           Address Line 1: 212 North Main Street_____
           Address Line 2: Suite 2203_____
        City, State, Zip: Dallas_____  TX 75012_____
                  Country:
                    Phone: 214/228-1000____ Date 00/00/00   type date as mm/dd/yy

              User Fields-              Remarks-
                    1: _____       _____
                    2: _____       _____
                    3: _____       _____
```

Fig. 16-6/MailList
screen.

```
              A D D   N E W   R E C O R D S          B:WS2LIST.DTA
  ┌─────────────────────────────────────────────────────┬──────────────┐
  │  ^Copy from previous record    ^Write/save record in file │ ^Get help    │
  │                                                     ├──────────────┤
  │                                                     │ Escape       │
  └─────────────────────────────────────────────────────┴──────────────┘
                    Type data and press Return.


    Record Number: 00004  Arvin Ritz

First, Initial, Last: Arvin_____ __ Ritz_____    Mr./Ms.: Mr._____
              Title: _____

           Company: _____
     Address Line 1: 8181 East 18th Circle_____
     Address Line 2: _____
   City, State, Zip: Pueblo_____  CO 86613____
           Country: _____
             Phone: 303/887-8679____  Date 00/00/00   type date as mm/dd/yy

       User Fields-                 Remarks-
               1: _____    _____
               2: _____    _____   Fig. 16-7/MailList
               3: _____    _____   screen.
```

As you complete typing each record, type

^W

followed by Return to save it. When you're finished, type

^W

to save the last record and press the Esc key when the MailList screen is blank. Take note, however, that pressing the Esc key when a record is on the screen will not save that data.

**Locating Records by Record Number—**MailList offers several options for locating specific records after you've typed them. One way is by record number. This method assumes that you know which record number you want to see or that you want to see them sequentially. To do this, type

L

from the MailList menu to Locate records by number. MailList then asks you to type a number. When you press Return, the record appears on the screen. Four command choices are shown at the top of the screen. Here are the first two:

^Previous/^Next number

Typing ^P displays the previous record in the file. Typing ^N displays the next record. The third selection is

^Erase record

Typing ^E lets you erase the currently displayed record. However, it is not automatically erased. A new menu appears on the screen, making it nearly impossible to accidentally erase a record. The three choices you have after giving the erase command are as follows:

```
Remove the data from the file by pressing R.
Return to the form and continue with Spacebar.
Return to the MailList menu with Esc.
```

Only the first choice, pressing

```
R
```

actually removes the record from the file.

The fourth choice on the Locate menu is

```
^Write/save modified record.
```

Remember that you can edit the records when they are displayed on the screen. If you have made any changes, you want to be sure to type

```
^W
```

to save the changes.

**Sorting the Records**—When records are first typed, they appear in record number order in the data file. However, when you give the sort command, the records are rearranged into a new order in the data file. This moves them from being in record number order to being in the order you specified.

As mentioned earlier, you might want to put the records in zip code order if you are printing letters, labels or envelopes that will be mailed. This means that during printing, MailList and MailMerge will read the records in the data file in order by zip code. If you are printing a telephone list, you'll likely want the list printed in alphabetical order based on the name of the company or individual. This sort command makes it possible for you to put records in this specific order.

You see the nine possible choices for sorting records when you type

```
S
```

from the MailList Menu. These are:

```
Name
Location
Date
Company
Zip Code
Record number
1st user field
2nd user field
3rd user field
```

MailList sequences the sorting. For example, when you sort the data file by name, the last name is sorted first, then the first name, followed by the middle initial and finally the company. Names will be listed in alphabetic order when you sort by zip code. For example, if you sort the list based on the zip code, Mr. Adams with zip code 85710 will print before Dr. Johnson and Ms. Williams whose zip codes are also 85710.

Keep in mind that the records can be sorted as many times as you want. You can sort the same data file in different ways by copying the file to another file with a different name. For example, the TOUR-LST.DTA data file you created could be copied to another file by typing

C

for Copy at the WordStar 2000 Opening Menu. You will copy from TOUR-LST.DTA to a file called *ZIP-TOUR.DTA*. The new file could be sorted in zip code order, leaving the original file in the record number order as typed.

**Viewing and Editing the Records**—When you have typed records in a data file, you can look at them and edit them. One of the ways is to recall the records in record number order. Another way is to use the View command. To do this type

V

for View and edit records from the MailList Menu. The first record in the file appears on the screen as you typed it. The View and Edit Menu gives you five command choices. Four of the commands are the ones you saw earlier on the Locate Records by Number Screen. To display other records in the data file type

^N

to see the Next record or

^P

to see the Previous record. They will be displayed in the order in which they were typed if the records have not been sorted and if no filter has been specified.

If, for example, the records have been sorted into zip code order, the first record you see is the one with the lowest zip code number. As you repeat the Next command, you will see the records displayed in a zip code sequence, regardless of the order in which you actually typed them.

**Using a Filter**—The fifth option on the View and Edit Menu asks you to type

^C

to Create or change the record filter. The filter lets you select a certain subset of records to be displayed during View and Edit. For example, let's say you are concerned only about records in the data file where the state is Wisconsin. When you type

^C

MailList displays the screen with asterisks filling all of the fields. To select only the Wisconsin records for viewing, press Return until the cursor is in the state blank. Then type

WI

the abbreviation you used for Wisconsin. Now when you move through the data file, only records with the state WI will be displayed. Type

^U

to Use the filter you typed. The record filter you specify will be in effect until you display and erase it by typing

^E

followed by

R

or until you exit the MailList data file. MailList will only display the records that match the typed filter.

When viewing records, you can make corrections by moving the cursor through the fields and retyping entries. Save the changes by typing

^W

to Write the revised record to the disk. This is the same command you used earlier when originally typing the record.

## USING MAILLIST DATA FILES WITH MAILMERGE

When the data file has been created with MailList, you can use it with MailMerge just like you used the data files in the previous chapters. A major difference is that each MailList data record always has 27 fields. You must include the names of all of the fields following the Load command in the MailMerge document.

For help with the order of the variables in the data file, use WS2LIST.FRM, one of the files on the Advanced Features disk. When you create a document to be printed with a data file created with MailList, select WS2LIST.FRM as the format.

The command area of this file includes the following merge information.

```
[ASK FOR datafile WITH PROMPT "What is the data file name?"
MAXIMUM LENGTH 40]
[CONDITION datafile=""]
[MESSAGE WS2LIST.DTA will be used.]
[USE WS2LIST.DTA FOR datafile]
[END CONDITION]
[SELECT DATA FILE &DATAFILE&]
[REPEAT UNTIL END OF DATA]
[LOAD DATA x, number, full-name, first, mi, last, Mr-Ms,
title]
[LOAD DATA company, addr1, addr2, city, state, zip, country]
[LOAD DATA phone, date, x, user1, x, user2, x, user3]
[LOAD DATA remark1, remark2, remark3, x]
```

This MailMerge command area will ask you for the name of the data file. If you do not supply one, it assumes you want to use WS2LIST.DTA, the default MailList data file name. Then note that the WS2LIST.FRM file names the 27 variable names. These are the names you will use in the text portion of the MailMerge document unless you give the Load command and type different variable names.

## PREPARED MAILLIST PRINTING FILES

MailList provides six files with MailMerge commands designed to read the data from files typed with MailList. These files are convenient because they contain all of the commands necessary to do a special kind of printing. If, however, they don't exactly match your printing needs, you can edit them, adding or deleting variable names you want printed.

To print one of these MailList files, press

P

at the Opening Menu and select the one to print. Respond to the questions on the Print Menu. WordStar 2000 prompts for the name of the data file you want to print.

**PROOF.LST**—The PROOF.LST file prints all of the information contained in each record. As its name suggests, you can use this for proofing the data records before you actually print labels or letters.

**PHONE.LST**—The designers of MailList also assumed that you might frequently print names and phone numbers from the data file. They prepared the PHONE.LST file to help you. It also prints the record number.

**LABEL.LST, LABEL3.LST, LABELXL.LST**—These three files are designed specifically for printing labels. LABEL.LST prints standard 3-1/2 by 1-inch labels. The LABEL3.LST document prints the same size labels but includes commands for printing them 3-across on the page. If you are using 5x3-inch labels, you can use the LABELSXL.LST file.

**ENVELOPE.LST**—This file is used for printing envelopes. It is designed to pause after printing each envelope. During the pause you can put another envelope into the printer.

# 17 Using StarIndex

After typing a report or research paper, you may need to number headings and subheadings and prepare a table of contents. You may also want a list of figures, tables and appendices. A longer work or a book requires an index. These are tasks StarIndex, one of the components of WordStar 2000 Plus, can do for you.

You mark entries for the table of contents, lists and indexes in the document as you type—or after typing is completed. The commands you use are on the Index Menu shown in Figure 17-1.

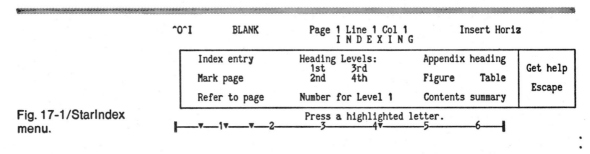

Fig. 17-1/StarIndex menu.

The second step is to run the StarIndex program, as you'll see later in the chapter. StarIndex reads the commands you have typed in the document. In the process it creates three new files in addition to your original document file. The first is the same as the original file but contains the text of the document with headings numbered as indicated by the StarIndex commands. Another contains the index entries and page numbers for the document. If you did not mark any entries for an index, this file is created but is empty after running the StarIndex program. The third file contains the table of contents entries and page numbers. This includes lists of figures, lists of tables and the appendix names.

## CREATING A TABLE OF CONTENTS

To create a table of contents you mark headings with StarIndex. These might be chapter or section names and lesser division headings in the document. StarIndex numbers headings as you want them and uses these markings for creating a table of contents.

**Marking Headings**—For example, let's say that the first heading you want to mark is the name of the first chapter. Position the cursor on the line where the name of the chapter will print in the document and type

^OI

for Option Index followed by a number from 1 through 4. To mark it as a major, level-1 heading, you type

1

and press Return. StarIndex displays bracketed words

[LEVEL-1]

[LEVEL-1]

on the screen with the cursor on the blank line between. You will type the name of the level 1 heading between the brackets. Type the name of the first chapter

CURRENT TRENDS IN TRAVEL PLANNING

and press the Down Arrow twice to move cursor past the bracketed command markers. You typed the name of the chapter in capital letters. It will be printed in capital letters in the document and in the table of contents. All chapter titles in the document will be level 1 headings. The next headings in each chapter are level-2 headings.

Let's say that you type several paragraphs of the document and now want to mark a level-2 heading. Position the cursor at the point, type

^OI2

and the command brackets

[LEVEL-2]

[LEVEL-2]

appear on the screen with the cursor on the blank line between them. You type the name of the level-2 heading

Needs of the Business Traveler

and press the Down Arrow twice to move the cursor past the command marker.

After typing more text, you may have another level 2 heading. Give the command again

`^OI2`

then type the name of the heading

`Needs of the Vacation Traveler`

and use the Arrow Keys to move the cursor outside the command brackets. Note that you need to type the capitalization of the heading as you want it to print in the document and in the table of contents.

As the document continues you'll need a level-3 heading. Position the cursor and type

`^OI3`

Then type the heading between the markers

`Outside the US`

and press the Down Arrow twice. And finally, you have two level-4 headings. Type

`^OI4`

followed by

`English-Speaking Countries`

and press the Down Arrow twice. Type

`^OI4`

again followed by

`Non-English-Speaking Countries`

and move the cursor outside the brackets.

**Marking Multi-line Headings**—So far, all of the headings you typed were one line. However, StarIndex does not limit you to one-line headings. If the text you type between the heading level markers is more than one line long, StarIndex recognizes it as a multi-line heading. It will print the heading on several lines in the document and in the table of contents.

**Marking Existing Headings**—Inserting StarIndex commands as you type is probably the easiest way to use them. However, sometimes you may unsure about the levels you want to assign to headings as you're typing. In this case you may find it more convenient to type the document, then edit it to add the StarIndex commands.

Let's say, for example, that you have typed the section entitled *CURRENT TRENDS IN TRAVEL PLANNING.* You typed the headings as you want them to appear in the document and in the table of contents. Now you want to go back to insert the StarIndex commands. To do this, position the cursor where the heading will print, type the desired level command, in this case

`^OI1`

so the

[LEVEL-1]

[LEVEL-1]

brackets again appear on the screen. The cursor is on the blank line between. Although the name of the heading already appears, it is necessary for you to type the name between the markers so StarIndex can recognize it. Type

CURRENT TRENDS IN TRAVEL PLANNING

and press the Down Arrow twice. Now the section title appears in duplicate. You need to remove the title you typed first—the one that is not between the command brackets. Place the cursor on the line and type

^RE

or press Shift-F6. In summary, if the heading already exists, you must give the desired level command, type the heading between the markers and remove the first heading text you typed.

**Marking Figures and Tables**—If your document contains figures, photos, drawings, tables or other similar items that should also be listed in the table of contents, you can mark them with StarIndex commands. When you run StarIndex, it automatically numbers the items and compiles lists for the table of contents complete with title and page number.

To mark a figure, position the cursor where the figure number and title are to print and type

^OIF

for Option Indexing Figure. A pair of bracketed words with the cursor on the blank line between again appears on the screen

[FIGURE]

[FIGURE]

Type the name of the figure on the line between the brackets. Then move the cursor outside the brackets with the Up or Down Arrow Key. When you run StarIndex, the figures are automatically numbered.

Tables are marked in much the same way as figures. Position the cursor where the table title and number are to print and type

^OIT

for Option Indexing Table. Again, a pair of bracketed words appear on the screen

[TABLE]

[TABLE]

with the cursor on the blank line between. This is where you type the name of the table. When you're done typing, move the cursor outside the command brackets by pressing the Up or Down Arrow Key. When you run StarIndex the tables are automatically numbered.

**Marking Appendices**—An appendix is also easily marked to be included in the table of contents. Position the cursor at the point in the document where the title of the appendix is to print and type

```
^OIA
```

for Option Indexing Appendix. Again a pair of brackets appears on the screen

```
[APPENDIX]
```

```
[APPENDIX]
```

With the cursor on the line between the brackets, you'll type the name of the appendix. StarIndex names the appendices alphabetically. The first is Appendix A, the next is Appendix B and so on.

**Adding Entries**—You can add additional table of contents, heading, index, and appendix entries anywhere in the document, inserting them between existing commands if you wish. If you have already run the StarIndex program, you will need to run it again so the changes will be properly ordered and numbered.

**Deleting Entries**—Sometimes you might want to delete an entry you have typed. To do this, be sure the display is turned on so you can see the command markers. Then remove the line between the bracketed words by positioning the cursor on it and typing

```
^RE
```

or Shift-F6. When the text is removed, StarIndex will ignore the command markers as well.

**Adding Table of Contents Comments**—To make the table of contents more useful to the reader, you can add explanatory text. Although you type the text in the document, it prints only in the table of contents.

Suppose, for example that you want to give the reader an idea of the topics covered in the first chapter of the BOOKLET document. To type the explanatory text, position the cursor below the level-1 heading command in the first chapter of the document. If necessary, turn on the display so you can locate the correct place. Then type

```
^OIC
```

the Option Indexing Contents summary command. You see a pair of brackets on the screen

```
[CONTENTS SUMMARY]
```

```
[CONTENTS SUMMARY]
```

With the cursor between the bracketed commands, you can type the desired text:

```
This survey of current trends provides insights into the needs
of business and vacation travelers in both English and
non-English-speaking countries.
```

When you have typed the comment, again move the cursor outside the brackets using the Arrow Keys.

## CREATING AN OUTLINE

You can easily create an outline giving the StarIndex commands and typing the text. When using this method for typing outlines, you do not type the numbers or letters marking the levels. StarIndex will do this for you.

For example, to help you write the first chapter, you could prepare an outline. When the display is on, the outline looks like this.

```
[LEVEL-1]
CURRENT TRENDS IN TRAVEL PLANNING
[LEVEL-1]

[LEVEL-2]
Needs of the Business Traveler
[LEVEL-2]
[LEVEL-2]
Needs of the Vacation Traveler
[LEVEL-2]
[LEVEL-3]
Outside the US
[LEVEL-3]
[LEVEL-4]
English-speaking Countries
[LEVEL-4]
[LEVEL-4]
Non-English-Speaking Countries
[LEVEL-4]
```

After running StarIndex, you print the BOOKLET.BOD file containing the outline using the OUTLINE.STY style provided by WordStar 2000 (more on these later in this chapter). StarIndex can number it in the usual outline format. You will need to add the desired indentations.

I. CURRENT TRENDS IN TRAVEL PLANNING

A. Needs of the Business Traveler

B. Needs of the Vacation Traveler

1. Outside the US

a. English-speaking Countries

b. Non-English-Speaking Countries

## CREATING AN INDEX

StarIndex also capably creates an index from marked entries in a document. An index is a useful addition to nearly any lengthy document, allowing the reader to quickly locate information that is more specific than the table of contents entries.

Let's say, for example, that you want to index the section *CURRENT TRENDS IN TRAVEL PLANNING.* You decide how to include the entry in the index so the reader will be able to locate the topic. The entry *Travel Planning* with the subentry *trends in* is your choice. To mark a word for indexing, position the cursor at the word and type

`^OII`

for Option Indexing Index. WordStar 2000 asks

`Index entry?`

and you type

`Travel Planning`

and press Return. Then WordStar 2000 prompts

`Subentry?`

so you type

`trends in`

and press Return again. When you see

`Boldface page number? N`

press Return to accept the No answer. When you want the page number printed boldfaced, you type

`Y`

then press Return. The index entry you have marked looks like this when the command display is turned on

`[INDEX ENTRY Travel Planning SUBENTRY trends in]`

Notice that you were never asked to type the page number for the indexed item. Later when you run StarIndex, it automatically assigns the page numbers. StarIndex notes the page number of the index entry when the index is created. For this reason, it is necessary to put the index command on the line with the entry being indexed or on a blank line preceding or following the entry if you prefer.

This way, you will be certain the index prints the correct page number for each entry.

**Multiple Index Entries on a Line**—Sometimes you need to mark more than one item on a line for the index. This is no problem for StarIndex. Give the index command once

`^OII`

and type the desired entry and subentry. Without moving the cursor to a new line, give the same command again followed by the entry and subentry.

**Quickly Marking Entries**—If you need to mark an entry repeatedly throughout a document, giving the indexing command and the typing the entry name can become cumbersome. For example, in the sample BOOKLET document you might index *Travel Planning* repeatedly. Let's look at a way to reduce typing and speed the index marking process. You'll do this by coupling the Locate command with the indexing commands you just learned.

With the cursor at the beginning of the document to be indexed, type

`^L`

the Locate command. When WordStar 2000 asks

`Word to locate?`

type

`travel planning`

WordStar 2000 locates the first occurrence of *travel planning* and marks it with the cursor. Move the cursor to an adjacent blank line and type

`^OII`

the index command. When WordStar 2000 asks

`Index entry?`

type

`Travel Planning`

using initial capital letters the way you want the index entry to print. Press Return. Press Return again when the question

`Subentry?`

appears because you don't want to specify a subentry. Press Return a third time in response to the question

`Boldface page number? N`

to accept the *No* answer.

You have now defined the index entry for *travel planning*. To use it repeatedly, you'll remove it here, store it in the Undo buffer and recall it as needed. To do this type

`^RE`

to Remove the Entire line or press Shift-F6. Then, before moving the cursor, give the Undo command by typing

`^U`

or by pressing F2. The entry is restored and a copy of it is retained in the buffer. Now you're ready to find the next occurrence of *travel planning* in the document. Type

`^N`

which is the Next command. The cursor stops on the next occurrence of *travel planning*. Give the Undo command again by typing

^U

or by pressing F2. This restores the index entry information in the document. By repeating the Next and Undo commands, you can locate and index all of the remaining occurrences of *travel planning*.

## ADDING CROSS REFERENCES

Another thing StarIndex can do for you is reference another page that has further information about a topic. This cross reference appears in the document, not in the index. Let's say, for example, that in the BOOKLET document an entire section is devoted to information about travel in Europe. Then at another place in the document, you briefly mention travel in Europe and you want to refer the reader to the more complete description. You can do this by using two StarIndex commands.

**Marking a Page**—The first thing you do is mark the page that has the detailed information about travel in Europe. Position the cursor at the point you want referenced and type

^OIM

for Option Indexing Mark. WordStar 2000 responds with

Mark page with what name?

so you type

Europe

and press Return. When you turn on the display you see

[MARK PAGE Europe]

**Referencing a Page**—Once a page is marked it can be referenced repeatedly elsewhere in the document. The page number of the referenced page can be printed within another sentence. For example, you may want a sentence to read: *See page 6 for more information about travel in Europe.*

Begin typing the sentence

See page

followed by

^OIR

the Option Indexing Refer to page command. WordStar 2000 then asks

Page to refer to?

You'll not type the specific page number; that's the job of StarIndex. Rather, you type the name you typed earlier when you marked the page. In this example you type

Europe

and press Return. The code WordStar 2000 inserts is

```
[REFER TO PAGE Europe]
```

When you run StarIndex, the page number is inserted into the document for you.

## RUNNING STARINDEX

So far in this chapter you have learned about marking text with StarIndex commands. When marking is complete, you finish the process by running the StarIndex program. This inserts the heading level commands as you specified and creates the table of contents and the index.

To run StarIndex, return to the Opening Menu and type

```
I
```

to select the Index option. If you want to display the Index choice, press the Spacebar at the Opening Menu. The lower portion of the menu then reveals the WordStar 2000 Plus options, one of which is StarIndex.

WordStar 2000 then asks

```
Document to index?
```

Type the name or move the highlight bar to the desired document and press Return.

**Selecting a Style**—Next WordStar 2000 asks

```
Style file to use?
```

If all of the style files are on the Drive B disk or on the hard disk, their names are displayed. Here are samples of the table of contents prepared with each of the styles:

**Outline Numbering Style**—OUTLINE.STY

```
                    Table of Contents


    I. CURRENT TRENDS IN TRAVEL PLANNING....................1
       A. Needs of the Business Traveler...................1
       B. Needs of the Vacation Traveler..................1
          1. Outside the US...............................1
             a. English-speaking Countries...............1
             b. Non-English-Speaking Countries...........1
```

## Simple Numbering Style—SIMPLE.STY

Table of Contents

## Compound Numbering Style—COMPOUND.STY

Table of Contents

## Manuscript Numbering Style—MSCRIPT.STY

Table of Contents

## Unnumbered Style—NONUMBER.STY

```
                    Table of Contents


    CURRENT TRENDS IN TRAVEL PLANNING....................1
       Needs of the Business Traveler.......................1
       Needs of the Vacation Traveler.....................1
          Outside the US...................................1
             English-speaking Countries......................1
             Non-English-Speaking Countries................1
```

Move the highlight to the desired style and press Return. When you have selected the style, StarIndex begins reading the document, creating the headings, table of contents and index according to the StarIndex commands you typed. The selected StarIndex style affects only the numbering and formatting of the items marked with StarIndex commands. The style or format of the document itself is unchanged.

**Using StarIndex with Floppy Disks**—If you are using StarIndex on a computer with two floppy disk drives, copy the desired style files to the disk in Drive B—the one with the document to be indexed. Do this before giving the Index command at the Opening Menu.

After selecting the Index choice at the Opening Menu and the style, you'll see a message on the screen saying that the INDEXWS2.EXE cannot be found. At this point remove the WordStar 2000 program disk from Drive A and insert a copy of the Advanced Features disk.

**Files StarIndex Creates**—When you run StarIndex, you'll find three new files on the disk in addition to the BOOKLET file you originally typed. Notice that the document name stays the same for each of the files StarIndex creates, but the extension changes to identify the contents of the new file.

**Document File (BOOKLET.BOD)**—This file is nearly like your original BOOKLET document except that BOOKLET.BOD file contains the headings numbered according to the style you selected. StarIndex read and acted on the commands you typed. This is the file you will print for the completed project.

**Index File (BOOKLET.IDX)**—If you marked entries for an index, you will find them in the BOOKLET.IDX file on the disk. You can see this document on the screen by choosing it after giving the Edit command from the Opening Menu. The index will be printed in two columns on the page with the subentries below the main entries and the page numbers in place.

**Table of Contents File (BOOKLET.TOC)**—All of the headings and comments you marked in the document are included in the BOOKLET.TOC file. The pages of the table of contents are numbered with lowercase Roman numerals—i, ii, iii, etc. The table of contents also includes the list of figures, tables, and appendices.

# 18 *Using TelMerge*

For years you have used the Postal Service to send documents to other people. It is not a simple process, but one that is easy to master. When you mail a letter, you know several days will elapse before it arrives. Worse yet, there is always the possibility it will get lost in the mail. Electronic mail eliminates that delay and uncertainty. You send a document over the telephone lines and it arrives at its destination within seconds. You can confirm immediately that it has been received. Like regular mail, electronic mail is not a simple process but is easy to master.

Because the people receiving your electronic mail might not be available or might be using their computer for something else at the time you want to send your document, many people use telecommunication services. Some of the well-known services include The Source, CompuServe, and EasyLink. You can think of these services as the equivalent of post office boxes. You send a document to them electronically and they store it in their computer's memory. The people to whom you sent the letter can "check the mail" at their leisure by calling the service and retrieving it.

Another option offered by communications services is hardcopy delivery. In this case, the service actually prints the document and delivers it to the recipient. They charge you for the delivery and for the time you spend connected to their service.

There are many aspects to telecommunications with a microcomputer. This chapter will not teach you everything there is to know about telecommunications.

That would take a whole book. What this chapter *will* teach you is how to easily send and receive electronic mail using TelMerge. If you are using a telecommunications service, you will also have to know how to use that particular service's commands and menus. You should refer to their documentation to learn that.

## WHAT YOU NEED TO START

Before you can consider using TelMerge, there are two prerequisites you must meet. You must have an appropriate modem properly hooked up to your computer, and you must subscribe to a telecommunication service or have access to a bulletin board system.

**Modems**—Your computer is not intrinsically capable of connecting to the telephone lines. To do this, you must have a special peripheral known as a *modem*. A modem changes the *digital* signals of the computer into *analog* signals the phone can use. The modem TelMerge supports is the Hayes Smartmodem, a very common modem also copied by many other manufacturers. If your modem is not a Hayes but is advertised as *Hayes compatible,* it will probably work with TelMerge.

Take note that not all telephone equipment can be connected to a computer. For example, the Centron system does not allow data communications. If you have a special phone system or PBX, you may need a regular line for the modem. If in doubt, contact your telephone service or equipment supplier.

Your phone line also should not have the *Call Waiting* feature. The clicking on the telephone line created by this feature can interfere with the telecommunication, causing you to lose information.

**Telecommunication Services**—Before you can use a telecommunications service, you must subscribe to it. You can do this in several ways. The easiest way is to call them and register. Here are the current phone numbers of the most popular services:

| | |
|---|---|
| CompuServe | 800/848-8990 |
| EasyLink | 800/527-5184 |
| ITT Telex and Timetran | 800/922-0184 |
| MCI Mail | 800/624-2255 |
| | (202/833-8484 in Washington, DC) |
| Official Airline Guides | 800/323-4000 |
| | (800/942-3011 in Illinois) |
| OnTyme Messaging Service | 800/227-6185 |
| RCA Telex and TELEXTRA | 800/526-3969 |
| The Source | 703/734-7500 |

**Bulletin Boards**—In addition to these, there are hundreds of other communications services. One popular and inexpensive type of service available throughout the country is the Bulletin Board System (BBS). Bulletin boards are usually free and are operated by volunteers in every major city and town. They usually feature a message system for electronic mail and a file transfer system for programs. Note that TelMerge can transfer programs only if they are in ASCII format.

**Direct Connect**—In addition to BBSs and telecommunication services, you can connect with other computers. If the other computer is also running TelMerge, you can transfer both ASCII and binary (program) files.

## USING ELECTRONIC MAIL

Once you have met the two prerequisites, there are five steps to using electronic mail:

1) Prepare a control file for each service you intend to use. This is only done once for each service or BBS.

2) Prepare the document you are going to send.

3) Connect with the service or BBS.

4) Send or receive a document.

5) Disconnect from the service or BBS.

**Preparing the Control File**—There are certain things TelMerge must know about a communications service before it can communicate with it. For example, it needs to know the phone number of the service and your password. It also needs to know the speed—or *baud rate*—to send information, how the other computer expects to receive it, and other technical information.

The things TelMerge needs to know about each service are contained in *control files*. Control files are unformatted Wordstar 2000 files—that is, they are created using the UNFORM.FRM format—arranged in a particular way. Each line in the file must begin with a TelMerge *keyword*—a specific command that tells TelMerge how to interpret the parameter that follows. After the keyword is a space or tab and a parameter.

**Understanding Keywords**—What the actual parameter is depends on the keyword. For example, the keyword

BAUD

can be followed by the parameter

1200

to indicate a speed of 1200 baud, or by

300

to indicate a speed of 300 baud. If no baud rate is specified, 300 baud is assumed. Each of the keywords has a default or assumed value if it is not specified.

An example of the contents of a Control File is shown in Figure 18-1. Here is what each of the lines in Figure 18-1 means:

**CLS**—This tells TelMerge to clear the screen when you begin this session.

**Say CompuServe Information Service**—The word Say displays a message on the screen, in this case CompuServe Information Service.

**Service CIS**—It tells TelMerge which service you are using.

```
CLS
Say              CompuServe Information Service
Service          CIS

Number
Userid
Password

Hardcopy         NO
Logfile          CIS.LOG
Logging          OFF
Baud             300
Port             COM1
```

Fig. 18-1/Example control file.

**Number**—You will fill in the telephone number of the service after the keyword `Number`, so TelMerge can dial it for you.

**Userid**—You can fill in your User Identification number, if needed.

**Password**—Almost every communication service requires a password to begin using it. When you subscribe to the service, you will receive a password. You should put it here, following the keyword `Password`. When you are using the service, pressing F6 will send your password as though you typed it at the keyboard.

**Hardcopy NO**—It tells TelMerge you do not want a printout of the telecommunications session. If you change the `NO` to `YES`, the printer will print whatever appears on the screen. You can also turn hardcopy on and off with F8.

**Logfile CIS.LOG**—If you turn logging `ON` in the next item, TelMerge will keep a complete record of the telecommunications session in the file listed here. If the file already exists, the existing file will be renamed *CIS.SAV* and logging will still occur.

**Logging OFF**—This tells TelMerge whether to send a record of the telecommunications session to the logfile. If you used `ON` for the parameter, logging occurs. If you use `OFF`, as in this example, logging will not occur. You can also turn logging on and off with F7.

**Baud 300**—This keyword tells TelMerge how fast to send data. 300 is the default.

**Port COM1**—The keyword `Port` tells TelMerge which communications port the modem is attached to—COM1 or COM2.

There are 40 possible keywords you can use in a Control File, but it is not necessary for you to learn them all. To try to explain each one and teach you how to program with them is beyond the scope of this book. The quick-and-easy way to use TelMerge is with the ready-made Control Files. If you decide to program control files, you can refer to the *TelMerge Reference Guide* in the *Advanced Features Guide.*

**TELMERGE.SYS File**—The most important Control File is TELMERGE.SYS. When you first access TelMerge, it looks for this file on the disk and executes it.

TELMERGE.SYS is provided on your disk, but you do not necessarily have to use it. The one provided allows you to choose a variety of telecommunications services. If you only use one service on a regular basis, you can rename TELMERGE.SYS something else. I suggest *OLDTEL.SYS*. Then rename the file relating to the service you use *TELMERGE.SYS*. Each time you access TelMerge, it will then automatically call your service.

If you use several services, you can call them by keeping the TELMERGE.SYS file on the disk, and simply adding your local telephone numbers and your passwords into the control files provided. The files provided are:

| | |
|---|---|
| CIS | Accesses CompuServe |
| ESL | Accesses Western Union EasyLink |
| ITT | Accesses ITT Telex and TIMETRAN |
| MCI | Accesses MCI Mail |
| OAG | Accesses Official Airline Guides |
| ONT | Accesses OnTyme Messaging Service |
| RCA | Accesses RCA Telex and TELEXTRA |
| SOU | Accesses The Source |
| STD | A generic control file you can change to allow you to access any other service or BBS |

After subscribing to a telecommunications service, you will receive a package of information. In it will be your password, a phone number to call to connect with them (usually a local telephone call), and a User ID if needed. You can add this information to the appropriate Control File by typing

E

at the Opening Menu and typing the information in beside the corresponding keyword.

**Customizing Control Files**—For example, suppose you wish to contact the Tucson IBM User Group BBS, which is 602/742-5187. Assume also that you have already been assigned the password *Public*. You could change the STD file to reflect your needs. It's a good idea to copy the file first, then change the copy so the STD file will still be available to use as a model for other control files in the future. To copy the file, type

C

on the Opening Menu. When WordStar 2000 asks

File to copy from?

type

STD

and press Return. In answer to

File to copy to?

type

TUC

followed by Return. The new file TUC will be a duplicate of STD.

Now that you have a file created, you can edit TUC to contain the information TelMerge needs. Figure 18-2 shows what you see on the screen before you edit the file.

```
CLS
Say           User-Defined Service

Netword
Hostid

Service       STD

Number
Userid
Password

Hardcopy      NO
Logfile       STD.LOG
Logging       OFF
Baud          300
Port          COM1
```

Fig. 18-2/Control file before editing.

As you can see, this is a generic file without a phone number. Move your cursor down to the word User and type

Tucson IBM PC User Group

deleting the words User-Defined Service. Where the control file has the word Service, change STD to TUC. Move your cursor after the word Number and put in the telephone number 1-602-742-5187.

If you are in area code 602, you do not need to put in 1-602-. Change the name of the Logfile to

TUC.LOG

If you are using a 1200 baud modem, you can either change the baud rate to 1200 or leave it as it is. This particular BBS supports both speeds. The entries for Network, Hostid, Userid and Password do not need to be changed. Later, you can put in a password if you wish. They are optional on this BBS.

The contents of the file should now resemble Figure 18-3.

```
                           CLS
                           Say          Tucson IBM PC User Group

                           Network
                           Hostid

                           Service      STD

                           Number       1-602-742-5187
                           Userid
                           Password

                           Hardcopy     NO
                           Logfile      TUC.LOG
                           Logging      OFF
                           Baud         300
                           Port         COM1
```

Fig. 18-3/Control file
after editing.

Now save this file with

^QS

or Alt-1. If you want to use this file with the TELMERGE.SYS file provided, you can add it to the menu. First, type

E

at the Opening Menu and edit TELMERGE.SYS. Then type

^L

to Locate

STD

in the file and replace it with

TUC

to save the file.

    If you want to include several user-defined control files in the TELMERGE.SYS file, you will have to do some advanced editing of the file. The boxes and lines in the menu are not necessary for its operation so can be deleted to make room for the new control files you wish to add. The actual appearance of the screen does not matter. It is only for your information and has no bearing upon the operation of TelMerge. The important part follows the menu—the four lines for each control file you wish to have available. The lines for the TUC control file look like this:

```
if =TUC
include TUC
end
endif
```

You can set up as many telecommunication systems control files as you like by adding similar lines to each you wish to access from this TELMERGE.SYS file. Now you are ready to prepare a document for transmission.

**Preparing the Document**—Documents sent over the telephone with TelMerge must be unformatted. The first way is to create a document using the UNFORM.FRM format. The second way is to create a file using any format but to print it to disk before transmitting.

**Unformatted Format**—The UNFORM.FRM format file disallows use of many of WordStar 2000's features including automatic centering, controlled page breaks, and special print commands. It is, however, the quickest of the two ways to create an ASCII file for TelMerge. After giving the Edit command at the Opening Menu and naming a file, select the UNFORM.FRM format. Then create the file. For example, you might want to type a short message such as *This is my first test of using TelMerge on a Bulletin Board System,* which you can later send to the TUC BBS.

**Printing to Disk**—If you select some other format for your file, you will have to print to disk before transmitting the file over the phone. This step takes more time than using UNFORM.FRM but has the added convenience of being able to use automatic centering, justification, forced page breaks, and other WordStar 2000 features. *However, many formatting features such as underlining will be lost when you print to disk and will not be transmitted over the phone.*

To print a document to disk, create and save it. Then at the Opening Menu type

P

and select the document you want to send. On the Print Decisions Screen, press Return in response to the first six questions. However, on the seventh question

`Send document to Printer or ASCII Disk File?`

type

D

for Disk file. WordStar 2000 asks you for the name of a file to send the document to. Type a name. I suggest you use the file extension *.TEL* to indicate that the file is meant to be telecommunicated. The new .TEL document is in ASCII format ready to transmit.

**Connecting with a Service or BBS**—When you have created a control file and a document, you are ready to access a communications service. If you have an external modem, be sure it is turned on. Then type

A

at the Opening Menu. TelMerge will be loaded and you will be prompted to choose a communications service. Type the three-letter identifier of the service—such as TUC—and press Return. TelMerge will take over from there, dialing the phone number and connecting you with the service.

Once you are connected with the telecommunications service, you will have to know something about how to use their menus and commands. If you have subscribed to a commercial service, its documentation will tell you how to use it. The WordStar 2000 commands are not in effect. If you are calling a BBS, you will find they are usually self-documenting through their menu systems. If in doubt about what to do next, you can usually type

HELP

or enter a question mark. The only thing in effect from WordStar 2000 is the set of Function Keys.

**TelMerge Function Keys**—Use of the Function Keys varies depending on the service. Most of them are standardized according to the list below. But watch out—they may change when you use another service. The meaning of each of the Function Keys is usually displayed at the bottom of the screen.

| | |
|---|---|
| F1 | You can define this key to be whatever you desire, using the "Function" keyword. |
| F2 | You can also define this function key to suit your needs. |
| F3 | DIR displays the disk directory. |
| F4 | SEND commences sending a document to the remote service. |
| F5 | USER ID sends your User Identification to the service. |
| F6 | PASSWORD sends your Password to the service. |
| F7 | LOG turns logging on and off. |
| F8 | HARDCOPY turns hardcopy—the printer—on and off. |
| F9 | BREAK sends a special signal called a *break* to the service. Some services use this to interrupt display of menus and text. |
| F10 | HANGUP hangs up the phone—it disconnects the modem from the telephone connection. |

**Logging and Log Files**—When you are using a service, you have the option of *logging,* which means that everything that appears on your screen will also be stored in a file. This is very useful when you are using a service for the first time. Press F7 to turn on logging. That way all the help screens and menus you use will be recorded. You can print them out later at your convenience. Then the next time you use the service you will not have to ask for the Help menus. Another benefit is reduced phone bills because you'll be connected for a shorter time. However, be sure that you have plenty of room on your disk—a log file can become quite long. A 30-minute session on a BBS can completely fill up a floppy disk at 1200 baud.

You specify the name of the log file in the control file. For example, you might have a log file named TUC.LOG. If that file exists when you start a new session, it will be renamed TUC.SAV and the file TUC.LOG will contain the new session. If both TUC.SAV and TUC.LOG exist on the disk, the old TUC.SAV will be deleted.

**Transferring Documents**—When you have connected with the telecommunications service or BBS, you must use its internal commands or menus to navigate to the correct place for sending or receiving your documents.

**Sending Documents**—When you have entered the appropriate commands, the service will usually prompt you with a message like Begin sending. At that point, you can press F4 and TelMerge will ask you for the name of the document to send. Type the name and press Return. The document will be sent to the remote location and then you can continue your telecommunications session.

**Receiving Documents**—Receiving documents is even easier. When the telecommunications service is ready to send you a document, just press F7 to begin logging. Don't press F7 if you are logging already. The Function Key is a toggle—pressing it once turns it on, pressing it again turns it off. Unfortunately, there is nothing on the screen to tell you whether you are logging or not. You must keep track.

One way you can sometimes tell is by your disk activity. If your disk starts spinning intermittently, you are logging.

The documents you receive are stored in the log file listed in the control file for the service you are using. After you finish telecommunicating, you can edit that file like any other. If you received more than one document, you can separate them into individual files. Mark each as a block and then write it to a new file by typing

^BW

the Block Write to file command.

As mentioned earlier, the only type of document you can't send or receive is a binary file. Binary files include programs and files created by some software. The only time you can send a binary file is when you are connected to another computer that is also running TelMerge and when you both have specified TelMerge as the service in your control file. In that case you can also send WordStar 2000 documents with formatting intact.

**Disconnecting from a Service or BBS**—When you have sent or received a file, you may transfer more documents or end your session. All telecommunications services have a method of leaving the service. There is always a menu choice to exit or there is a command to leave—usually *Goodbye, G* or *Bye*. You should avail yourself of the correct command to leave. However, if you don't know the command, you can press F10 to hang up the phone.

When the telecommunications session is finished, you will be prompted to press any key. That returns you to the WordStar 2000 Opening Menu. You're now ready for your next task.

# Index